"The Jesus Chronicles"
A Chronological Study Through the Gospels
Volume 1

"The Jesus Chronicles"
A Chronological Study Through the Gospels
Inductive Bible Study
Volume 1

Copyright © 2013 by Morningstar Christian Chapel
Published by Morningstar Christian Chapel
ISBN: 978-1-940198-00-2

Additional Copies of this book are available by contacting:

Morningstar Christian Chapel
Whittier, CA 90603
562-943-0297

Printed in the United States

Unless otherwise noted all Scripture quotations
are taken from the New King James Version,
Copyright © 1982 by Thomas Nelson, Inc.

Revision 1c

The Jesus Chronicles Inductive Bible Study

Volume 1

This study guide is part one of a two part Inductive Bible Study series based on the book "The Jesus Chronicles" by pastor Jack Abeelen.

Morningstar Christian Chapel Inductive Bible Studies are designed to help believers go through the Bible and discover the rich Truths of God's Word for themselves. Paul told Timothy to be a student of the Word (2 Timothy 2:15) and Peter encouraged us to have an answer for every man who asks for the hope that lies within us (1 Peter 3:15).

These studies are not designed to replace your weekly involvement in your local church fellowship for Bible study but are rather to supplement your daily devotions and reading times before the Lord. God promises to teach us much if we desire to know Him (Jeremiah 33:3).

These studies are used by Morningstar to lead Men's and Women's Bible studies. They also make an excellent resource for anyone wishing to lead a small group.

May God bless you as you study and meditate upon His wonderful Word and especially here through the Gospels as we focus on Jesus our Lord.

Lesson Index

Lesson	Page
Introduction: Jesus of Nazareth: Luke 2:39–52	1
Section I: The First Year Of Ministry	
1. Handling Temptation: Luke 4:1–13	5
2. Invited to a Wedding Feast: John 2:1–11	9
3. Jesus and Nicodemus: John 3:1–36	13
4. Imagine Meeting You in a Place Like This: John 4:1–42	17
Section II: The Second Year Of Ministry	
5. The Healing of the Nobleman's Son: John 4:43–54	21
6. Jesus Goes Home: Luke 4:13–30	25
7. Follow Me!: Mark 1:14–20	29
8. A Day in the Life of Jesus: Luke 4:31–44	33
9. Cleansing, Healing, and the Opposition: Luke 5:12–26	37
10. A Sick Tax Collector: Mark 2:13–22	41
11. Jesus at Bethesda: John 5:1–15	45
12. Jesus Speaks to His Would-Be Assassins: John 5:16–47	49
13. Sabbath Day Controversies: Luke 6:1–11	53
14. Pressure, Prayer, and Provision: Mark 3:7–19	57
15. Poor in Spirit: Matthew 5:1–3	61
16. Mourning and Meekness: Matthew 5:4–5	65
17. Hungering, Thirsting, and Mercy: Matthew 5:6–7	69
18. The Pure, the Peacemaker, and the Persecuted: Matthew 5:8–12	73

the JESUS chronicles

Lesson	**Page**
19. The Church in the World: Matthew 5:13–16	77
20. The Christian and the Law: Matthew 5:17–20	81
21. Illustration 1: Murder Begins in the Heart: Matthew 5:21–26	85
22. Illustration 2: Adultery: Matthew 5:27–30	89
23. Illustration 3: Divorce: Matthew 5:31–32	93
24. Illustration 4 and 5: Oaths and Retaliation: Matthew 5:33–42	95
25. Illustration 6: Love Your Enemies: Matthew 5:43–48	99
26. How and Why I Do What I Do: Matthew 6:1–4	103
27. Lessons on Prayer: Matthew 6:5–15	107
28. Fasting: Food for Thought: Matthew 6:16–18	111
29. Your Treasure and Your Master: Matthew 6:19–24	115
30. Why I Don't Have to Worry: Matthew 6:25–34	119
31. Jesus on Judging: Matthew 7:1–12	123
32. How Do I Get to Heaven from Here?: Matthew 7:13–14	127
33. Beware of False Prophets: Matthew 7:15–20	131
34. Saying, Hearing, and Doing: Matthew 7:21–29	135
35. Who's the Boss?: Luke 7:1–10	139
36. The Widow of Nain Meets the Lord: Luke 7:11–17	143
37. Doubt and the Believer: Luke 7:18–23	147
38. Jesus Speaks of the Faithful and the Not So Faithful: Luke 7:24–35	151
39. Jesus Loves Sinners: Luke 7:36–50	155
40. The Unpardonable Sin: Mark 3:20–35	159
41. How Do You Hear?: Luke 8:1–15	163

Lesson	**Page**

42. He Spoke to Them in Parables: Matthew 13:10–17, 24–52	167
43. A Late-Night Boat Ride: Mark 4:35–41	171
44. Man of the Tombs: Luke 8:26–39	175
45. The Desperate Find Jesus: Luke 8:40–56	179
46. Another Opportunity Lost: Mark 6:1–6	183
47. Learning to Serve By His Power: Mark 6:7–13	187
48. Death of a Conscience: Mark 6:14–29	191
49. I'm Your Sufficiency: Mark 6:30–44	195
50. Storm Sense: Mark 6:45–56	199
51. Jesus: The Bread of Life: John 6:22–71	203
52. Truly Clean!: Mark 7:1–23	207
53. Jesus and Two Gentiles: Mark 7:24–37	211
54. Nurturing Spiritual Understanding: Mark 8:1–26	215
55. Who Do You Say That I Am?: Luke 9:18–26	219
56. The Transfiguration: Luke 9:27–36	223
57. True Greatness: Luke 9:37–50	227
58. The Stage Is Set: Matthew 18:1–14	231
59. Church Discipline: Matthew 18:15–22	235
60. The Parable of the Unforgiving Servant: Matthew 18:23–35	239

Introduction
Jesus of Nazareth: Luke 2:39-52

Always begin every Bible Study with prayer. It is the Holy Spirit Who is your Teacher!

1. Read Luke 2:39-52.

2. Read The Jesus Chronicles – Introduction: Jesus of Nazareth (pages xiv – xix)

What is Luke's focus in his Gospel, and how does it differ from the other Gospel accounts?

3. All good parents take great interest in their children's development: how tall they have grown already, how quickly they learned the alphabet or how far they can throw a baseball. Yet God's assessment of His Son focuses primarily on His spiritual growth. What are we told about Jesus' spiritual development?

We are given a couple of examples of men who did not focus on the spiritual growth of their children. What was the outcome in their lives?

a. 1 Samuel 2:12 & 17; 1 Samuel 3:12 - 13

b. 1 Kings 1:5 - 7

Indeed whatever our children's accomplishments might be in this life they pale in comparison to who rules in their lives. If they know the Lord, they will be fine; if not, the greatest worldly achievements won't keep them. What instruction are we given regarding how to raise our children in the ways of the Lord?

a. Deuteronomy 6:4-9

b. Proverbs 22:6

c. Ephesians 6:4

4. What happened when the days of the Passover celebration in Jerusalem were complete?

Where did Jesus' parents find Him? What was He doing?

How did those who heard His conversation respond to Him?

Jesus was absorbed in His learning, in His development and spiritual insight. Because Jesus was fully human, He had to grow. He grew in faith. What do we learn about Jesus' daily life following this event?

5. The word wisdom in Luke 2:52 speaks of spiritual insight. The word stature speaks of physical development. Jesus grew in the things of God. He grew in favor with God as His spiritual habits and practice, and understanding of His ways continued to develop. As Christians, we too should be drawing nearer to the Lord in our walks and then finding favor with others. The Gospel will offend people – we should not. What instructions are we given that will help us to increase in wisdom?

a. 2Timothy 2:15

b. 1Peter 2:1-3

c. 2Peter 3:17, 18

For these 18 years, Jesus was faithful at home, because that too fell under the category of being about His Father's business; it's both a matter of heart and a matter of diligence. Jesus is called "Jesus of Nazareth," but that denoted far more than simply being a reference to His hometown. It speaks of the character He developed there. Have you been about your Father's business? What is He preparing you for?

Chapter 1
Handling Temptation - Luke 4:1-13
(Matthew 4:1-11; Mark 1:12-13)

Always begin every Bible Study with prayer. It is the Holy Spirit Who is your Teacher!

1. Read Luke 4:1-13.

2. Read The Jesus Chronicles Chapter 1 (Pages 1-7).

3. Jesus' public ministry began with His baptism. He traveled from Nazareth to the Jordan River in the south where John was baptizing. According to John 1:19-36, what was John's ministry and what did He declare about Jesus?

   What does Romans 6:1-4 teach us about the meaning of baptism in the life of the believer?

4. Luke 4:1 begins with the word "then", which attaches Jesus' confrontation with the Devil directly to Jesus' baptism, the preceding event. What happened after Jesus was baptized, filled with the Holy Spirit, and declared to be the Son of God?

   Who led Jesus into the wilderness?

   What was the purpose of this testing?

   What is the purpose of trials in our lives?

　　　a. Romans 5:3-5

　　　b. 2Corinthians 4:16, 17

　　　c. 1Peter 1:6, 7

　　　d. James 1:2-4

　　What words of encouragement and promise are found in John 16:33?

5. Walking with Jesus in this world does not promise ease or comfort; there will be hardship, and there will be trials. The walk can be a difficult road, but the Lord has a purpose and has given us a promise of victory. What do you learn about the manner in which the temptations will come in your life from this account of Jesus in the wilderness?

　　How does the description of life in the world from 1John 2:15-16 compare with the temptations Jesus faced in the wilderness?

　　What was Jesus' one defense through each of these temptations?

　　How then will we find victory when faced with temptation from the enemy?

a. Deuteronomy 8:1-3

b. Hebrews 4:12-16

c. Psalm 119:130

We are told in Luke 4:13 that the enemy departed from Him...until an opportune time. Satan's vacations are short, but God's victories are eternal. How do you plan to face the next temptation that comes your way? Jesus had victory because He fully relied on the power of the Holy Spirit and completely obeyed God's Word. Will you do so today?

8

Chapter 2
Invited to a Wedding Feast
John 2:1-11

Always begin every Bible Study with prayer. It is the Holy Spirit Who is your Teacher.

1. Read John 2:1-11.

2. Read The Jesus Chronicles Chapter 2 (Pages 8-13).

3. John wrote in his gospel that his purpose for writing was to make sure the reader understood that Jesus is the Lord and that when one believes in Him, one finds eternal life. To that end, He chose eight specific miracles around which to build his case. According our text, what was the first miracle?

Why do you think our Lord chose this particular setting for His first recorded miracle?

Do you think this speaks to the importance of the marriage commitment?

What does the Bible teach us about the marriage bond?

a. Genesis 2:21-24

b. Matthew 19:4-6

4. Wine was a staple in the culture of the day, and being a good host was of utmost importance. In Scripture, whenever wine is associated with spiritual things, it always speaks of the joy the Lord gives. However, some use this truth to justify drinking of alcohol. How do the following Scriptures warn against the bondage that comes with alcohol abuse?

a. Leviticus 10:1-11

b. Romans 14:14-16

c. Proverbs 23:29-35

It is commonly thought that Mary, Jesus' mother, was the wedding hostess and that, this wedding was perhaps that of a close relative. When they ran out of wine and Mary brought this dilemma to Jesus' attention, what was His response?

Why did Jesus say, "My hour has not yet come"? What might Mary have hoped would happen at this public event?

5. So often we want God to work in our time frame rather than waiting on His perfect timing. How are you encouraged to wait by watching Mary's gracious acceptance of God's timing at this wedding?

What do we learn from the following exhortations about the importance of patiently waiting?

a. Isaiah 40:28-31

b. Psalm 27:14

What instruction did Mary give to servants at the wedding feast?

It is important to note that these are the last recorded words of Mary, Jesus' mother. What important lesson can we learn from her instruction?

What lesson can we learn from the actions of the servants in completing the task? Why do you think the Bible says they filled them up to "the brim"?

According to Colossians 3:23, how are we, as believers, to serve Jesus each day?

Jesus took the ordinary and made it extraordinary at this wedding feast. He is still doing so in lives today! Has He taken your ordinary life and transformed it? He wants to! Will you allow Him to?

Read 2Corinthians 5:15-21. How will you live it out in your life today?

Chapter 3
Jesus and Nicodemus
John 3:1-36

Always begin every Bible Study with prayer. It is the Holy Spirit Who is your Teacher.

1. Read John 3:1-36.

2. Read The Jesus Chronicles Chapter 3 (Pages 14-24).

3. In context, Jesus had been working miracles and preaching the Gospel and had recently cleansed the Temple in Jerusalem. Nicodemus was a devout man who had spent his entire life in religious service yet he realized he lacked some basic answers in his life. When did Nicodemus come to see Jesus? Why?

How does Nicodemus approach Jesus?

It is interesting that Nicodemus never even gets to ask a question of Jesus. What does this teach us?

In verses 3, 5, and 7, Jesus essentially says the same thing. What vital instruction does Jesus give to the elderly spiritual leader in Jerusalem and to every person throughout history, including those living today?

What does it mean to be "born again"?

The words "water" and "of the Spirit" must be taken together because they are the method by which people come to God. Can you explain what Jesus meant by His statement, "unless one is born of water and the Spirit, he cannot enter the kingdom of God"?

How do the following Scriptures describe this born again experience?

a. 2Peter 1:2-4

b. 2Corinthians 5:17

c. Ezekiel 36:26, 27

4. In John 3:16 we find what is probably the best-known verse in the Bible. It is the entire Gospel in 25 words. How does this verse describe what is required to have true salvation?

What does John 3:16 clearly teach us about God's heart, God's mind, and God' will?

What does Acts 4:12 teach us about the vital Gospel message?

Because Jesus came, we are obligated to respond to His coming and to look to Him because we have been bitten by sin. It isn't that Jesus came to pass judgment. Judgment had already come. If we do nothing, we are already condemned. Jesus came to provide the answer for our condemnation. He paid the penalty for our every sin. Why, then, do many people not get saved?

5. Beginning in John 3:22 we read the account of John baptizing in Aenon near Salim. The growing number of people coming to Jesus frustrated some of John's disciples. How did John view this issue?

What can we learn and apply to our lives from John's surrender to God's will and plan for his life?

It is very difficult in Greek and in the context of the chapter (3:31) to determine whether this is John the Baptist continuing his preaching or whether this is John the Apostle's commentary. What important point is being made in John 3:31-33?

Every word out of Jesus' mouth was 100 percent God's Word without flaw or error. If you want to see the kingdom of heaven, what must you do?

Every person is required to make a personal choice. Re-read John 3:16 and 36. Have you decided to trust Jesus? Who do you need to tell?

Chapter 4
Imagine Meeting You In A Place Like This
John 4:1-42

Always begin every Bible Study with prayer. It is the Holy Spirit Who is your Teacher.

1. Read John 4:1-42.

2. Read The Jesus Chronicles Chapter 4 (Pages 25-36).

3. Jesus left Judea and travelled north toward the Galilee. Why did He decide to go north? Why did He go through Samaria rather than the well-travelled route crossing the Jordan and then back into the Galilee in the north?

   What are we told in John 4:4 that reveals the compassionate heart our Lord has for the lost?

   Jesus and the disciples arrived in Sychar at noon. Jesus was weary from the journey. Who did He meet at Jacob's well?

   Why might it have been necessary for her to travel to the well at noon rather than early in the morning?

   This Samaritan woman arrives with an attitude only to find Jesus just waiting to reach out to her. The lesson from her encounter with Jesus is that you cannot fall so low that you can't be reached and saved. What were Jesus' first words to her?

What does He mean by "living water"?

4. As we see often throughout the Gospels, Jesus met this woman right where she was and began to share with her about her need. How did He pinpoint her need in John 4:13-15?

According to John 4:16-19, what next essential step did Jesus take to reach this woman?

How does Romans describe the state of all mankind apart from God?

a. Romans 3:23

b. Romans 5:12

The Samaritan woman was brought face to face with God's knowledge of her life and her failure. What was her reaction?

What lesson can we learn from watching how Jesus dealt with this woman who was broken by her sin and exposed by His love?

5. When the truth of her sin hit home, what evasive tactic does the woman try in John 4:20?

She wanted to talk about where to worship, but Jesus told her how true worship was accomplished. What did He say?

Then this lonely, empty-hearted woman began to talk about the Messiah (the Christ), how did Jesus respond to here expectation?

The woman by this time really had no way to argue. Unfortunately, at this point the disciples return with lunch. They marveled that He even spoke to a Samaritan woman. They had no idea of the transformation that was taking place. She left her water pot, went into the city and made a bold declaration. What did she ask?

Take note of the transformation that took place in this woman's heart by recording the titles by which she addresses Jesus.

a. John 4:9

b. John 4:11

c. John 4:19

d. John 4:29

What was the first thing this new woman did as she headed back to town after meeting Jesus?

According to 2Corinthians 5:17-20, how are we described as new believers in Christ, and what is our new mission and calling?

The disciples returned with food, but Jesus tells them, "I have food to eat of which you do not know." Do you want to be revived? Start reaching out to others with the Gospel. Jesus was completely satisfied after this spiritual encounter with the woman at the well, and He began discussing the spiritual harvest. What does He say about the harvest in John 4:35?

What do we learn about the importance of teamwork in evangelism?

According to John 4:40-42, what was the amazing outcome of this trip to Samaria where Jesus knew He "needed" to go?

How will it affect your willingness to reach out in faith and boldness to the seemingly unreachable? Will you start today?

God has much to be done. Whom will He use? It can be you!

Chapter 5
The Healing of the Nobleman's Son
John 4:43-54

Always begin every Bible Study with prayer. It is the Holy Spirit Who is your Teacher.

1. Read John 4:43-54.

2. Read The Jesus Chronicles Chapter 5 (Pages 39-44).

3. After ministering to Nicodemus and the Samaritan woman, Jesus headed for the Galilee, where He began His second year of ministry. What event had recently occurred in the Galilee that drew Jesus to this region?

What was Jesus mission and message in the Galilee?

According to John 4:44, what kind of receptions did Jesus expect He would receive in the Galilee?

What did the Galileans say about Jesus as recorded in Matthew 13:54-57?

Why would Jesus leave a hungry people and a thriving ministry in Samaria to face rejection in His home country?

What do we learn from Matthew 4:12-17 about Jesus' motive for heading home?

4. The welcome Jesus initially received in Galilee had nothing to do with the message He preached. Why were they interested in seeing Jesus?

How is this tragically-wrong motive still at work in the lives of people today who are seeking "signs and wonders" and who are not willing to surrender their lives to the Savior of the world?

In the midst of many people looking to be entertained, one man with budding faith stood in the crowd. Who was he and what was his request?

Why did He come to Cana? How did his motives differ from the crowds in town?

It is true that the Lord uses "signs and wonders" to attract people to Him, but this is not to be the end result. Why and how are we to come to Jesus?

What does the writer of Hebrews tell us about this saving faith?

a. Hebrews 4:2

b. Hebrews 11:6

5. According to John 4:50, how did Jesus respond to the request of this broken-hearted Roman father?

What immediately happened in this father's heart?

How is the faith of this Roman nobleman displayed in his reaction to Jesus' instruction?

Did he run as fast as he could back to Capernaum? Or did He rest in Jesus' promise of healing?

When was the boy healed?

While the town looked for miracles, this nobleman looked for God. Are you looking to Jesus for what He can give you or how He can entertain you? Or do you truly want to know Jesus Christ, the Savior of the world, and most importantly, your Savior?

How did the faith of this nobleman affect those of his household? Why?

How does Psalm 103:17, 18 help explain the how the transforming faith of one can save generation after generation?

Read the story of another Roman believer in Matthew 8:5-13. What is the same? What is different?

What lesson that can we apply to our walk with Jesus today?

Chapter 6
Jesus Goes Home – Luke 4:13-30
(Matthew 13:54-58; Mark 6:1-6)

Always begin every Bible Study with prayer. It is the Holy Spirit Who is your Teacher.

1. Read Luke 4:13-30.

2. Read The Jesus Chronicles Chapter 6 (Pages 45-51).

3. What kind of reception did Jesus receive when He returned home?

   What was one of His first stops?

   Why do you think it was His practice to go first to the synagogue?

   What do we learn from the custom or pattern Jesus followed about the importance of gathering together with other believers on a regular basis?

   What instruction are we given in Hebrews 10:25?

   Have you made it your custom to regularly gather together with the saints? If not, you need to begin to do so.

On the day Jesus entered the synagogue and was asked to read the Scripture, what passage was He given?

What declaration did He make?

4. It is important to note that this prophecy from Isaiah, which was written in 683BC, teaches us that even Jesus did not minister in His own strength. How was He able to accomplish the ministry He was sent to do?

We have a similar calling in our lives today. What do the Scriptures say about our calling and ministry?

a. Matthew 5:14-16

b. 2Corinthians 5:18-21

According to Acts 1:8, what is the only way we can be effective in the ministry we have been called to do?

What does it mean when Isaiah 61 says Jesus preached the Gospel to the poor?

How does Matthew 5:3 define this person Jesus describes as "poor"?

How is this point made clearer in Matthew 9:10-13?

According to Luke 7:19-23, what was Jesus' response to the men John sent to inquire about Who He was?

5. What bold statement did Jesus make in Luke 4:21?

What was the reaction of His crowd?

Sadly, Jesus' charm captivated them, but their wonder clashed with His familiarity. They admired His words but they weren't affected by them. They admired His style, His attitude, and the way He presented Himself—but the things He said didn't affect their hearts. The invitation of the Gospel is personal. It requires a decision. Will you follow Him fully and whole-heartedly or not? There is no room for walking the fence. What is the lesson from the story of the widow in 1 Kings 17?

How can you apply it to your walk of faith today?

How did the meager faith of Naaman in 2 Kings 5 compare with that of Jesus' hometown neighbors in Nazareth?

The citizens of Nazareth had heard enough from Jesus. What was their response?

It is tragic when background, church tradition, and pride keep anyone from faith in Jesus. What does He declare about Himself in John 14:6?

What challenge did Joshua give to the children of Israel in Joshua 24:15?

The personal question that requires a personal answer is, "Who will you serve?"

Chapter 7
Follow Me! – Mark 1:14-20
(Matthew 4:12-17; Luke 4:14-15)

Always begin every Bible Study with prayer. It is the Holy Spirit Who is your Teacher.

1. Read Mark 1:14-20.

2. Read The Jesus Chronicles Chapter 7 (Pages 52-58).

3. With great determination Jesus headed north to the Galilee. During the first year of His public ministry He ministered mainly to individuals. What were His mission and ministry like during the second year?

What was the general response of the hearers?

According to Mark 1:15, Jesus went north preaching a very succinct message. What was it?

What are the three points of salvation Jesus declared?

1.

2.

3.

How can you apply this 3-point outline in your conversations with friends, family, and neighbors?

A lot of people conclude they are Christians because they go to church. Is this enough? What is the true necessary requirement for salvation?

4. In our text we witness the calling of four disciples. Who are they? How did they respond to Jesus' invitation to follow Him?

What do we learn about their familiarity with Jesus and His ministry from John 1:29-45?

How long had Simon, Andrew, James, and John known about the ministry of Jesus?

By observation, how does the Lord most often reach individuals?

Who shared Jesus with you? When did you decide to follow Him?

5. We don't know for certain how long these men traveled with Jesus or how often they spent days or weekends with Him. We do know they went back to work because here at the beginning of Jesus' second year of ministry, they are still running their fishing business. Can you imagine the personal cost involved for them to follow? What do we learn from the following Scriptures about the call and cost of discipleship?

a. Matthew 10:37-39

b. Philippians 3:7, 8

What can we tell about the size of the crowd that was now following Jesus from Luke 5:1-3?

After preaching from Peter's boat, what instruction did Jesus give to Peter in Luke 5:4?

How large was the catch?

What was Peter's response to this obvious miracle?

On this amazing day these four fishermen went from knowing about Jesus to actually knowing Him. They were promoted from fishermen to fishers of men. As Christians, this too is our calling! How do the following references describe this calling?

a. Matthew 5:14-16

b. 2Corinthians 5:17-20

c. 1Peter 2:9

Have you responded to Jesus' calling in your life to wholly follow Him? Don't be satisfied with just knowing about Jesus. Instead, be sure that you're at the place where you would leave everything behind to follow Him.

Know this, God wants to bring you closer.

Chapter 8
A Day in the Life of Jesus
Luke 4:31-44

Always begin every Bible Study with prayer. It is the Holy Spirit Who is your Teacher.

1. Read Luke 4:31-44.

2. Read The Jesus Chronicles Chapter 8 (Pages 59-64).

3. What type of city was Capernaum? What type of reception did Jesus have here?

How did it compare to Jesus' birthplace of Nazareth?

What lesson do we learn about the Lord's ability to work in a place, or a heart, that is open to His coming?

Why is it that two people can attend, listen, and be exposed to the same teaching with completely opposite results?

According to Luke 4:32, how did the people respond to Jesus' weekly teachings in the synagogue?

We read that Jesus taught with authority. What does that mean? How do you think this was different from what the people were used to hearing?

According to Luke 5:30-32, what was Jesus' mission?

How did one group of guards react to Jesus' teaching according to John 7:46?

4. From our text, what rather unusual occurrence took place in the synagogue?

This is a vivid reminder that, as believers, we are engaged in active warfare against the enemy of our souls. What does 1Peter 5:8, 9 tell us about the enemy's mission and our method of success?

How can you have confidence of victory over the enemy's attacks in your life?

What do the following Scriptures teach us about the promise of certain victory over the enemy?

a. 2Corinthians 10:4-6

b. Ephesians 6:13-18

c. 1John 5:4, 5

5. According to Luke 4:36 & 37, what was the word around the city about the miracle that took place in the synagogue?

There was an "echo" or "buzz" that spread throughout the entire city. When the church is walking in Jesus, the city in which the church is planted ought to show the effects. What took place at Simon Peter's house?

What took place after sunset on that Sabbath day when the travel restrictions of the Law were lifted?

Why did the huge crowds seek out Jesus? How did He minister to them?

What distinction is made between those who were sick and those who were demon-possessed?

What important lesson do we learn by observing our Lord's prayer life in the midst of long ministry-pressured days?

According to Mark 1:35, why did Jesus go to a deserted place?

What pattern do we see in the following Scriptures?

a. Mark 6:46

b. Luke 6:12

The people pleaded for Jesus to stay. Why did He need to leave? What message did He have to share?

Personal: When you find yourself overwhelmed with busyness, do you pray more or less? What should you be doing?

Chapter 9
Cleansing, Healing, and the Opposition
Luke 5:12-26

Always begin every Bible Study with prayer. It is the Holy Spirit Who is your Teacher.

1. Read Luke 5:12-26.

2. Read The Jesus Chronicles Chapter 9 (Pages 65-69).

3. In the second year of His ministry, Jesus' popularity grew daily, but so did the opposition. According to Luke 5:12, who did Jesus meet?

Describe the leper's approach to Jesus.

What is leprosy a type of in the Scriptures?

Why is leprosy like sin?

What made this particular healing so unique?

Was there a demand or a command? Or was it with humble surrender that the leper fell at Jesus' feet?

What additional details do we find in Mark 1:40, 41 about Jesus' response to this leper?

Personal: Is there a sin in your life that you need to bring to Jesus in repentance? Will you be cleansed?
Or is there a trial or circumstance that you need to ask the Lord to "do whatever He wants to do?" Will you trust Him?

4. Jesus told this leper not to tell anyone. Why?

In contrast, as the church, what is our mission and calling?

a. Mark 16:15

b. Matthew 5:16

Jesus told the leper to "tell no one," but everyone knew! Notice that the busier Jesus got, the more He withdrew to pray. How does this example encourage you in your everyday walk with Jesus? Do you spend time daily with Jesus?

Why is it an absolute necessity that we do so?

a. Psalm 119:105 & 130

b. Hebrews 4:12, 13

c. 1 Thessalonians 2:13

d. 2 Timothy 3:16, 17

5. The Pharisees—or, literally, the "separatists" – were men who lived such outwardly religious lives that not only did everyone stand in awe of them, but also no one could even hope to be like them. They sat away from those seeking Jesus but close enough to hear something they might be able to use against Him. How do their actions stand in stark contrast to the friends of the paralyzed man?

What extreme action did they take?

Why did Jesus ask the question, "Which is easier, to say, 'Your sins are forgiven you,' or to say, 'Rise up and walk'?'"

Obviously this man was repentant because Jesus doesn't arbitrarily forgive those who won't repent. His words sparked an immediate response from those outside on "critics row". What accusation did they make against Jesus?

According to Luke 5:22, 23, we learn that Jesus knew what they were thinking. What did He do to prove He could both forgive sins and heal bodies?

What kind of faith brings God's forgiveness and mercy?

What kind of faith is God looking for from you?

Chapter 10
A Sick Tax Collector
Mark 2:13-22

Always begin every Bible Study with prayer. It is the Holy Spirit Who is your Teacher.

1. Read Mark 2:13-22.

2. Read The Jesus Chronicles Chapter 10 (Pages 70-74).

3. During Jesus' second year of ministry the crowds and the opposition increased. What unusual decision did Jesus make to distinguish the Good News of the Gospel from the religious ways of man?

What made Levi (Matthew) such an unusual choice to be a disciple?

What do we learn from Jesus' selection criteria?

What does 1 Samuel 16:7 teach us about how the Lord chooses?

What does Isaiah 55; 8, 9 add to your understanding of God's ways?

4. Our Lord chose Matthew because He knew He could take him and make of him what no one else could. Even if people despised and rejected him, God had a plan for him. The same is true of you, as His child. What do we learn from the following Scriptures about God's plan for those who follow Him?

a. John 15:15-19

b. Galatians 1:15

c. Ephesians 2:10

Upon seeing Jesus at a gathering of tax collectors, what was the consensus among the self-made religious leaders?

According to Mark 2:17, how did Jesus respond to their complaints?

How do we see religious bias exhibited within the church today?

5. In our text today we see a second illustration of the clash between "works religion" and grace. What question was asked in Mark 2:18?

What was Jesus' response to their inquiry?

There is a place for fasting in the life of the believer. What is the reason we ought to fast?

What do we learn about the true purpose for fasting from reading Isaiah 58:1-14?

What illustrations are given to us in Mark 2:21-22?

How do these illustrations apply to the subject of the Gospel of grace versus a religion of works?

You could describe Levi's (Matthew's) life as a new wineskin. How about yours? What will keep a new wineskin new – spiritually speaking?

There's a big difference between being religious and being saved. May we learn from Matthew the depth and length to which the Lord will go to take us in by His grace. Record Ephesians 2:8,9 and make it your prayer today that the Lord would allow you to walk and rest in His grace!

Chapter 11
Jesus At Bethesda
John 15:1-15

Always begin every Bible Study with prayer. It is the Holy Spirit Who is your Teacher.

1. Read John 5:1-15.

2. Read The Jesus Chronicles Chapter 11 (Pages 75-80).

3. One of the characteristics of the Gospels is the substantial amount of time devoted to the ongoing battle between religion and its adherents, and Jesus who came to call us to faith and a relationship with Him. How is the conflict highlighted in the account of Jesus' ministry in Bethesda?

What was the occasion that brought the crowds to Jerusalem?

Why might this feast be called the feast of the Jews rather than the feast of the Lord?

You can see the remnants of the pools of Bethesda today just outside of St. Anne's church. According to John 5:3, why were the masses gathered near the pools?

What was the reputation amongst the sick and hurting about this pool? Did healing really take place here?

4. In the shadow of the Temple, where the religious were trying to gain favor with God through their works, lay the masses of hurting people who hoped in vain superstition. Into their midst came the Savior of the world. What did Jesus ask this lame man?

What do you think He was truly asking of him?

How does this encounter illustrate the compassion and mercy with which the Lord seeks the lost?

How do the following Scriptures speak of Jesus' mission?

a. Luke 5:31, 32

b. Luke 19: 9, 10

c. John 6:44

d. 1John 4:9

5. Jesus knew this man's heart and the length of his suffering – a great reminder that the Lord always knows about you and your need. Salvation begins with God considering you – not with you considering Him. If Jesus waited for us to fully understand Him before touching our lives, no one would ever be saved.

The lame man responded to Jesus' question by declaring his inability to reach the water. We are not told of the state in the lame man's heart, but what is made clear by his obedience?

How do you think this man must have felt as he believed and stood up for the first time in 38 years?

In the midst of his joy, how did the religious men respond according to John 5:10?

According to Exodus 20:8-11, what was the purpose of the Sabbath Day?

The Jews had the written prophecies of the Old Testament regarding the coming Messiah. What does Isaiah 35 say about the miracles that would take place in that day?

When the Jews confronted this man about his action on the Sabbath, what was his response? How can you follow his example of simple faith when unbelievers challenge your obedience to Jesus?

Where did the healed man go first after being healed? Why?

Jesus found this man in the Temple. What did He say to him?

Use a Dictionary of Bible Words to define the word "well" in John 5:14.

When this man left Jesus, after having been made whole, what did he do?

If you are a believer in Jesus Christ today, you have been made whole. Are you faithfully declaring that it was Jesus who made you whole?

Chapter 12
Jesus Speaks to His Would-Be Assassins
John 5:16-47

Always begin every Bible Study with prayer. It is the Holy Spirit Who is your Teacher.

1. Read John 5:16-47.

2. Read The Jesus Chronicles Chapter 12 (Pages 81-86).

3. Imagine speaking face-to-face with powerful, religious men whose goal it is to murder you. What would you say? We are studying Jesus' longest discourse to date in the chronology of the Gospels, and it was delivered to those who wished to destroy Him. These religious men believed they could work their way to heaven and that they had no need for a Savior. They were wrong, and so are those today who are following in their religious pursuits. According to John 5:14-16, why did the Jews seek to kill Jesus?

Just think - these religious men had first-hand evidence of an amazing miracle, and yet they refused to believe. Jesus had just healed a man who had been lame for 38 years. What was their complaint about this healed man's actions?

What clear declaration of Deity does Jesus make in John 5:17-18? How do we know the Jews clearly understood His claims?

Jesus states that He is doing the work of His Father who never stops working. The religious Jews' complaint was that this miracle took place on the Sabbath, and the law was being broken. What is the true purpose of the Sabbath?

What does Mark 2:27-28 teach us about the Sabbath?

4. According to John 5:19-21, what do we learn about the relationship of God the Father and Jesus, His Son?

How did Jesus live and serve as He walked upon the earth?

Jesus told His would-be assassins that they hadn't seen anything yet. What word does He use in John 5:20 that speaks about the reaction of those who would soon see great and marvelous works by Jesus' hand?

What is the definition of the word marvel?

Read Luke 8:40-53; Luke 7:12-15; and John 11:43-44. Do these accounts cause you to marvel?

What do we learn from Deuteronomy 32:39 about Who has the power to kill and make alive?

Can you imagine how these well-taught Jews might have made a connection when Jesus said to them, "I can give life to whom I will?" Along with the giving of life, what do we learn from John 5:22-24 about Jesus mission on earth?

We still hear the same argument today, "I believe in God, but not Jesus." Write out John 5:22-24 below. How might it help you in sharing with someone who does not believe Jesus is God?

5. According to John 5:26, Jesus not only gives life but also is its source. The religious man points to his own performance and accomplishments. The believer points to Jesus, Who is life itself. What title does Jesus use for Himself in John 5:27?

What does Jesus mean in John 5:29 by the phrase "those who have done good?"

Death is not the end. Everybody's final destination depends on whether they have done good or evil—which is defined in God's Word as whether they have believed in Jesus as the Father's only provision for sin, or whether they thought they could take care of their sin on their own. There was plenty of evidence for these hostile men to believe. According to John 5:31-35, who was one faithful witness?

What is the second witness of Who Jesus is according to John 5:36?

When John baptized Jesus, the Father confirmed who Jesus was. Read Matthew 3:13-17. What were the Father's words?

Jesus called on John the Baptist, His own works, and the Words of the Father – Scripture itself—as witnesses to Who He was. The religious folks had the Word, but the Word didn't have them. It didn't move them. As a result, although God stood before them in the Person of Jesus, they weren't able to recognize Him. Jesus reminded these would-be assassins that the responsibility for their unbelief fell squarely on their shoulders. If you want to get right with God, what do you have to do?

Chapter 13
Sabbath Day Controversies
Luke 6:1-11

Always begin every Bible Study with prayer. It is the Holy Spirit Who is your Teacher.

1. Read Luke 6:1-11.

2. Read The Jesus Chronicles Chapter 13 (Pages 87-90).

3. In this second year of Jesus' ministry, the crowds gathered in record numbers. The people loved what Jesus had to say, but the religious leaders did not. Does this conflict still exist amongst the church today?

How would you describe the doctrine of "works righteousness?"

On the contrary, what does the Bible say about the righteousness of man?

How do the following Scriptures support your answer?

a. Romans 3:10

b. Psalm 14:2, 3

c. Isaiah 64:6

How are you able to enter the kingdom of heaven?

a. Romans 6:23

b. Romans 10:13

c. Romans 10:9, 10

4. One area of conflict that highlighted the works vs. grace debate was the application of the Sabbath Law. According to Luke 6:1-2, what question arose on the Sabbath day?

What is the command regarding the Sabbath according to Exodus 20:8-11?

What had the Pharisees done to this law to cause great confusion and even greater bondage?

How did Jesus respond to the question of "work" on the Sabbath in Luke 6:3-5?

5. According to Luke 6:6-7, what was the motive of the Pharisees and Scribes who constantly watched Jesus' every move?

What did they believe about Jesus' ability to help the sick and broken lives of those He encountered?

What question did He pose to the Pharisees in Luke 6:9?

What further details are we given in Mark 3:5-6 about the meeting between Jesus and the Pharisees?

What do we learn from the following Scriptures about Jesus' mission?

a. Matthew 18:11

b. Matthew 20:28

c. Luke 4:18-21

d. John 10:10-11

According to Luke 6:10-11, how did Jesus display His divinity to this group of hard-hearted "religious" leaders?

Did they believe? What did they do?

Chapter 14
Pressure, Prayer, and Provision – Mark 3:7-19
(Matthew 10:1-4; 12:15-16; Luke 6:12-19)

Always begin every Bible Study with prayer. It is the Holy Spirit Who is your Teacher.

1. Read Mark 3:7-19.

2. Read The Jesus Chronicles Chapter 14 (Pages 91-94).

3. As a growing number of people continued to come to Jesus, He took the next step in preparing His followers to be ready for the demands of being disciples. According to Mark 3:7, what did Jesus do and why?

Jesus' ministry began with His preaching of the message of repentance and declaring Himself the Savior to be followed. Who was coming to hear Him, what were they seeking, and how far did they travel?

Were they all seeking Jesus as their Savior, or did they have other motives?

How did Jesus treat each of them?

Just as it was with the crowds that followed Jesus in the Galilee, today there are many churches that boast of huge attendance and far reaching influence. Can we judge the true spiritual effectiveness of a group based on numbers?

Even the enemy recognized Who Jesus was, but many of those who sought Jesus in the Galilee went away as spiritually dead as when they had arrived. According to Mark 3:13, what decision did Jesus take to remove Himself from the crowd? Who did He take with Him?

4. Out of the thousands who followed Him, Jesus appointed and trained twelve. They became the foundation of the church. According to Luke 6:13, what title did He give to these twelve?

What is the definition of the title "apostle"?

Mark 3:14 tells us, Jesus "appointed" the twelve. What is the definition of the word that is translated appointed?

The job of these Apostles was two-fold. According to Mark 3:14-15, what were they to do?

5. God chose these men and they stand as a great example of the truth that the Lord can use anyone He picks as long as they surrender to His will. These men would not have made a top-twelve list of the most influential. But, they were chosen, and they were not mistakes, because God doesn't make mistakes. Why would the Lord choose men like these?

Have you ever considered that it might be impossible for God to use you because you feel unqualified? How does John 15:16 stand as an encouragement to you today?

What does Paul teach us in 1Corinthians 1:27-31 about the servants the Lord uses?

What do the following Scriptures add that will encourage you to step out in faith today?

a. Matthew 28:18-20

b. Acts 2:42

c. Colossians 3:16

d. Matthew 5:16

e. 1Peter 2:9

Thirty years later, Paul wrote in Colossians 1 that the Gospel had gone throughout the entire world. It began with this motley group of twelve. It continues today with you...He can use you mightily as you surrender to His will!

Chapter 15
Poor in Spirit – Matthew 5:1-3
(Luke 6:20-26)

Always begin every Bible Study with prayer. It is the Holy Spirit Who is your Teacher.

1. Read Matthew 5:1-3.

2. Read The Jesus Chronicles Chapter 15 (Pages 95-97).

3. During the second year of ministry and after choosing His twelve disciples, Jesus went to the mountain away from the multitudes and taught His disciples what we know as the Sermon on the Mount. The crowds were huge and the needs were everywhere. What was the constant message of the false teachers?

If you met with one of these false teachers what might they say you needed to do to get to heaven?

Have you met, or do you know, someone that today uses this same false reasoning about getting to heaven?

It was in the face of this false teaching that Jesus took His disciples aside to teach them the true and only way to enter into the Kingdom of God. What truth did He want them to fully understand?

To whom was this sermon delivered?

What are some of the topics that Jesus covered in this three-chapter sermon?

4. Record Matthew 5:3.

Summarize, in your own words, what Jesus meant when He said, "Blessed are the poor in spirit..."

What is the definition of the Greek word that is translated "blessed" in verse 3?

How does this amazing truth conflict with the opinion and beliefs of many "religious" people in the world today?

5. Poverty of spirit is a blessed place to be. How can a person get to this place?

How do the following examples reveal the heart of the one who is "poor in spirit"?

a. Luke 5:1-8

b. Isaiah 6:1-5

c. Matthew 8:5-8

According to Philippians 3:4-8, what was Paul's outlook about the importance of his credentials and accomplishments?

It is only when people see God face to face that they see themselves as empty. What does Isaiah 66:1-2 teach us about the quality of heart God is seeking?

What more do we learn about the one who is "poor in spirit" from the following Psalms?

a. Psalm 34:18

b. Psalm 51:17

Read Luke 18:9-14. Which man was "poor in spirit"?

Personal: How about you? Have you been bringing a list of "good works" in an attempt to satisfy the Lord, or are you blessed because you know you are "poor in spirit"? Write a prayer to the Lord telling Him about your poverty.

Chapter 16
Mourning and Meekness – Matthew 5:4-5
(Luke 6:20-26)

Always begin every Bible Study with prayer. It is the Holy Spirit Who is your Teacher.

1. Read Matthew 5:4-5.

2. Read The Jesus Chronicles Chapter 16 (Pages 98-100).

3. We cannot study the Beatitudes in isolation. They're all intertwined. In fact, even the order in which Jesus spoke them cannot be changed. Why it this true?

In review: How would you explain the meaning of Jesus' direction in Matthew 5:3 – "Blessed are the poor in spirit"?

If you realize you are poor in spirit, what will happen in your heart and spirit according to Matthew 5:4?

Read Matthew 19:16-22. How does the sorrow of this man differ from what Jesus is speaking about here in Matthew 5?

How does Romans 7:18 describe Paul's understanding of his spiritual state? When you consider your own life do you agree with his assessment?

4. What does Matthew 5:4 promise to those who are truly brokenhearted about the depth of wickedness in their lives?

What is the good news that brings comfort to the heart of the one who falls on the mercy of Jesus?

a. Psalm 34:18

b. Psalm 145:18

c. Isaiah 55:6, 7

d. Jeremiah 29:12, 13

When we find ourselves in a place of mourning over our bankrupted spiritual state and we find comfort and forgiveness through the finished work of Jesus Christ at Calvary, what are we compelled to do?

5. We have learned that these Beatitudes are like building blocks. According to Matthew 5:5, what fruit is produced in the heart of the believer who understands he has nothing to offer and runs to Jesus for comfort and healing?

How would you define the word "meek" in Matthew 5:5?

Does being meek mean that someone is a weak person?

How does Matthew 11:28-30 illustrate the answer to the last question?

What do we learn about meekness from the following Scriptures?

a. Psalm 25:9

b. James 1:21

How does meekness differ from being mild-tempered?

David dealt with King Saul in meekness. He had several opportunities to kill him but rather chose to trust the Lord to handle his enemy. How can you apply what you have learned about mourning and meekness to your walk with the Lord today?

Chapter 17
Hungering, Thirsting and Mercy
Matthew 5:6-7
(Luke 6:20-26)

Always begin every Bible Study with prayer. It is the Holy Spirit Who is your Teacher.

1. Read Matthew 5:6-7.

2. Read The Jesus Chronicles Chapter 17 (Pages 101-104).

3. What are the first three Beatitudes? Can you record them without looking?

The first three Beatitudes are designed to empty us. Beginning in Matthew 5:6, the Lord tells us of those things which are to fill us. What are we told in this verse?

How would you define "righteousness" from verse 5?

Who produces the desire to change in the heart of the believer?

The blessing of this Beatitude is found in the very process of hungering and thirsting. It is in the willingness to know and please God that we find that which we so desire – joy! What is the definition of the word "hunger" in Matthew 5:6?

Read Luke 15:11-24. How does the prodigal son's life illustrate the truths of the Beatitudes we have recently been studying?

4. According to 2Timothy 2:22, what important steps must we take in our lives to cooperate with the work of the Holy Spirit in our lives?

What pursuits and actions must we regularly practice in order to feed our hunger and thirst for righteousness?

What are some things that can hinder our pursuit or quench our thirst for righteousness?

What do the following Scriptures teach us about hungering and thirsting?

a. John 4:13, 14

b. John 6:48-51

c. Hebrews 12:1-3

d. James 1:21, 22

5. According to Matthew 5:7, what is the fifth Beatitude?

The first four Beatitudes deal exclusively with our relationship with God. We must empty ourselves to the point where He fills us with hunger to be more like Him. How are these next Beatitudes different from the first four?

How would you define the word "merciful"?

What does God's mercy protect you from?

What more do we learn about God's mercy and its effect on your walk with Jesus?

a. Micah 6:8

b. Colossians 3:12, 13

c. James 3:17

Mercy is a characteristic of the believer's life. Read Psalm 103:8-18. Write out a prayer of praise, and ask the Lord to use you today to extend His mercy to someone you meet.

Chapter 18
The Pure, The Peacemaker,
and The Persecuted – Matthew 5:8-12
(Luke 6:20-26)

Always begin every Bible Study with prayer. It is the Holy Spirit Who is your Teacher.

1. Read Matthew 5:8-12.

2. Read The Jesus Chronicles Chapter 18 (Pages 105-108).

3. The last three Beatitudes all begin with the letter "p". What are they?

   1.

   2.

   3.

Does the term "pure" mean sinless?

What does it mean to be "pure in heart"?

How does the phrase "pure in heart" speak to the motives and priorities in your life?

Read the parable of the sower in Matthew 13:18-23. Which ground represents the follower who is "pure in heart"?

What promise is made to the one who is "pure in heart" in Jeremiah 29:12 &13?

What promise is given in Matthew 5:8 to the believer who is "pure in heart"?

What does it mean when it says, "they shall see God?"

4. According to Matthew 5:9, what effect ought the believer have on the world in which he lives?

First and foremost an outgrowth of our salvation should be peace. According to Ephesians 6:15, what must the believer use in order to bring peace to the world?

What do we learn about this peacemaker from Isaiah 52:7?

How does 2Corinthians 5:18-21 encourage you to be bolder in your role as a peacemaker?

5. As we go forth bearing the precious Gospel to a lost world, we will, like our Lord, encounter much resistance and even persecution. What will be the direct result of sharing Jesus?

According to Matthew 5:10-12, who is blessed?

Why will the persecution come?

According to verse 12, how are we to respond when persecution comes? Why?

The suffering we are to endure is the suffering that comes from aligning ourselves with Jesus. What do we learn from John 15:18-20 about this persecution?

What does Peter add that will help you when you face persecution?

a. 1 Peter 3:13, 14

b. 1 Peter 4:12-14

What does 1 Peter 4:15 tell us about the wrong reason to bring suffering upon ourselves?

Think about the prophets and those who have gone before us in faith. Read Hebrews 11:32-40. Write a prayer of rejoicing because your reward is in heaven.

Many, many believers are dying daily in the world today simply for believing in Jesus Christ. Will you commit to praying for the persecuted church?

Chapter 19
The Church in the World – Matthew 5:13-16
(Mark 9:50; Luke 14:34-35)

Always begin every Bible Study with prayer. It is the Holy Spirit Who is your Teacher.

1. Read Matthew 5:13-16.

2. Read The Jesus Chronicles Chapter 19 (Pages 109-112).

3. The focus of the Sermon on the Mount is very clear. It is designed to delineate the difference between grace and works, between the Law that cannot make a person righteous and the Gospel that can. In Matthew 5:13-16, what are the two illustrations Jesus uses to talk about the influence of the believer in the world?

What do we learn about this influence from 2Corinthians 2:15-17?

Think about the term "fragrance of Christ" – does the love of Jesus in you draw others to Jesus, or cause them to reject Him?

What does 1Corinthians 1:17, 18 teach us about the message of the cross?

What is added in 1Corinthians 1:23, 24?

How are you encouraged from John 15:20?

4. We are called the "salt of the earth" in Matthew 5:13. Why would this have been a very familiar analogy to the disciples?

What are three attributes of salt that make it vital to life, and how do these truths apply to our ministry as the "salt of the earth"?

According to 2Thessalonians 2:6, 7, what is the role of the church while we await Jesus' soon coming?

What instruction are we given in Colossians 4:6?

Personal: Are your words saturated with grace and salt? Will you ask the Lord to increase your influence for Him amongst your family and friends?

5. Still focusing on the believer's influence in the world, how does Matthew 5:14 refer to the believer in Jesus Christ?

How does Jesus describe Himself in the following Scriptures?

a. John 8:12

b. John 9:5

From Matthew 5:14-16, what is the common truth about the light that we must take to heart?

Is it effective, then, to be a secret disciple?

In Matthew 5:16, when our light shines before men, what do they see and do?

What more do we learn about our ministry of being "the light"?

a. Romans 13:11, 12

b. Ephesians 5:8

c. Philippians 2:15, 16

Chapter 20
The Christian and the Law
Matthew 5:17-20

Always begin every Bible Study with prayer. It is the Holy Spirit Who is your Teacher.

1. Read Matthew 5:17-20.

2. Read The Jesus Chronicles Chapter 20 (Pages 113-116).

3. What is the intention of the Sermon on the Mount?

What are the three categories of the Law?

1.

2.

3.

What was the purpose of the Ceremonial Law?

What are we told in Matthew 5:17 regarding the reason for Jesus' coming?

How did His death at Calvary fulfill the Law?

What was the Judicial Law, and why was it given to the nation of Israel?

What are the principles encased in the Judicial Law?

4. Whenever God speaks of the effect of the Law, the reference is to the Moral Law of God. This Moral Law does not change. What is its purpose?

How does Paul describe his encounter with the Law in Romans 7:7-12?

How does Galatians 3:19-25 describe the purpose of the Law?

The difference between the religious person and the Christian is that the religious person will seek to keep the Law in his own strength then offer his best efforts to God as evidence of his good intentions. What would you say to a family member or friend who offers a list of "good works" as their ticket to heaven?

How does Romans 4:7, 8 encourage you in your walk today?

5. How does Matthew 5:19 speak of the practices of the scribes and Pharisees in Jesus' day?

Read Matthew 23:13-33. What is your impression of Jesus' strong rebuke to these "religious" men who misled the people?

What does Jesus say about the actions and values of the Pharisees in Luke 16:15?

The lesson of the Sermon on the Mount is that religion breaks God's Law. What does He require of those who follow Him?

What did Jesus mean when He said, "Unless your righteousness exceeds the righteousness of the scribes and Pharisees...?"

How do the following Scriptures clearly describe the way in which we must come to God?

a. Ephesians 2:8, 9

b. Romans 3:21-26

c. Romans 10:8-11

God's judgment against man's sin will be based on man's heart. Outward appearance means nothing to God. We must come to Jesus by grace through faith in Jesus Christ. We have nothing else to offer. What reminder do we find in Jeremiah 17:10 regarding the truth that nothing is hidden from the Lord?

Chapter 21
Illustration 1: Murder Begins in the Heart
Matthew 5:21-26 (Luke 12:57-59)

Always begin every Bible Study with prayer. It is the Holy Spirit Who is your Teacher.

1. Read Matthew 5:21-26.

2. Read The Jesus Chronicles Chapter 21 (Pages 117- 119).

3. How does a person get to heaven? This is the question that brought sharp discussions between Jesus and the scribes and Pharisees of the day. It is still the number one question asked today. Jesus gave the Sermon on the Mount with one purpose; what was it?

From God's standpoint, what is the purpose of the Law?

How did the religious leaders of the day misrepresent its purpose?

In Matthew 5:21, Jesus begins a series of examples to better define the true meaning of the Law. He begins by saying, "You have heard that it was said…" The Old Testament makes it clear that murder is sin. How does Jesus more clearly explain the meaning of this commandment with His statement that begins, "But I say to you…?"

The scribes and Pharisees applied the commandment only to outward behavior. Jesus teaches us that God looks at the motive of the heart that leads to murder. What are the sins of the heart that lead to us thinking of "murdering" someone?

4. In verse 22, Jesus refers to anger without a cause. When we are angry, most of us are certain we have a cause; however, what do we learn about righteous anger?

If you have righteous anger, Who are you protecting?

The minute our anger becomes one of protection of self and selfish interests, it is no longer righteous anger. What do we learn about anger in the life of believers?

a. Psalm 37:8

b. Proverbs 19:11

c. Ephesians 4:26

d. Ephesians 4:31, 32

e. James 1:19, 20

What is the difference between the two examples of anger Jesus gave in Matthew 5:22?

5. Whether the sin is a spontaneous eruption or a settled determination, the hatred in man's heart is irrefutable proof of his sinfulness, his violation of the law and his need for a Savior. What instruction are we given in Matthew 5:23 regarding our responsibility to make peace in our relationships?

Does it matter who is "at fault" in the division?

Praise, prayer, and worship all required a sacrifice in the Old Testament. In our walk with Jesus today as we bring our gift of worship, our hearts must be pure of sin for our gift to be received. Read the account of the Pharisee in Luke 18:9-14. What do you learn about the prayers God hears?

In Jesus' day, it was the plaintiff's responsibility to physically bring the defendant to court. What direction does Jesus give us regarding our obligation to seek peace in Matthew 5:25, 26?

What important teaching is added in the following Scriptures?

a. Romans 12:17-20

b. James 3:14-18

Chapter 22
Illustration 2: Adultery
Matthew 5:27-30

Always begin every Bible Study with prayer. It is the Holy Spirit Who is your Teacher.

1. Read Matthew 5:27-30

2. Read The Jesus Chronicles Chapter 22 (Pages 120-122).

3. The second example of how the scribes and Pharisees had rewritten the Law to accommodate their works concerned the issue of adultery. What is the Law of old?

What did Jesus say about adultery?

How do you define the word "looks" in Matthew 5:28?

How do you define the word "lust" in Matthew 5:28?

How does 2Samuel 11:2 -3 illustrate the truth that sin is already present in the lingering look?

4. The fact that a long, lingering look, or an entertained desire for that which is forbidden is sin reminds us that we are desperately in need of a Savior. How does James 1:14-15 describe this trap of temptation?

What is the origin of this temptation?

How do the phrases "drawn away" and "enticed" speak about a trap?

What is the end result of our yielding to the temptations in our lives?

What important reminder do we find in 1John 2:16-17?

How do the following Scriptures describe the victory over temptation that is available to the believer in Jesus Christ?

a. Galatians 5:24-25

b. Ephesians 2:1-5

c. Titus 2:11-13

d. Titus 3:3-7

5. What instruction does Jesus give in Matthew 5:29-30?

Was Jesus offering a physical solution to a spiritual problem?

What important point did Jesus make in these two verses? How would you explain it's meaning if someone asked you?

Jesus was not talking about self-mutilation. He was talking about self-examination. We need to be aware of what we look at and touch and be careful about where we go and what we do. He was telling us to do whatever it takes to keep from stumbling. How do the following Scriptures speak to the process of removing whatever will cause you to fall?

a. Luke 9:24-25

b. Romans 6:6-9

c. Romans 8:13-16

d. Galatians 5:24-25

Chapter 23 – Illustration 3: Divorce
Matthew 5:31-32
(Matthew 19:9; Mark 10:11-12; Luke 16:18)

Always begin every Bible Study with prayer. It is the Holy Spirit Who is your Teacher.

1. Read Matthew 5:31-32.

2. Read The Jesus Chronicles Chapter 23 (Pages 123-124).

3. On the subject of divorce, Jesus uses the same formula He used in the previous examples. According to Matthew 5:31, what was the teaching of the day?

What did Jesus say?

Read Deuteronomy 24:1-4. God gave this Law to Moses to protect women from indiscriminate divorce. What did the Law command?

According to Jesus, in Matthew 19:7-8, why did Moses give the commandment in Deuteronomy 24?

Jesus responded to the Pharisees' loaded question by taking them beyond the culture, beyond the argument of the day, beyond Deuteronomy 24 and back to the beginning. Read Genesis 2:24-25. What was God's perfect plan from the beginning?

4. Divorce is not God's will. Deuteronomy 24 was given as a concession to protect women from the abuse they were suffering at the hands of their husbands. What more do we learn about God's heart on the subject from Matthew 19:3-6?

What do we learn from the following Scriptures that, when taken to heart, will bring greater stability to the Christian family?

a. Malachi 2:14-16

b. 1Corinthians 7:10-11

c. Ephesians 5:31-33

5. Although the Pharisees made divorce merely a paperwork issue, Jesus said, "It's not a matter of writing. It is a matter of the heart." According to Matthew 5 and 19, Jesus said that because sexual immorality brings death to the marriage bond, it is the only reason that God allows divorce. What warning is found in Proverbs 6:32 about the long term effects of infidelity in a marriage?

Divorce is not the unpardonable sin. Divorce and adultery are both forgivable. How does John 8:3-11 illustrate this truth?

God's grace and mercy are offered abundantly to the repentant sinner; however, we need to be very careful not to abuse His grace. He knows our hearts! If you have fallen into sin, turn and repent. God will restore you. What promise is given to us in 1John 1:9?

Read Psalm 51. This Psalm is King David's prayer when the Prophet Nathan revealed David's secret sin. How does it encourage you in your walk with the Lord today?

Chapter 24
Illustration 4 and 5: Oaths and Retaliation
Matthew 5:33-42

Always begin every Bible Study with prayer. It is the Holy Spirit Who is your Teacher.

1. Read Matthew 5:33-42.

2. Read The Jesus Chronicles Chapter 24 (Pages 125-129).

3. According to Matthew 5:33, what was the common teaching of the scribes and Pharisees regarding the taking of oaths?

What is Jesus' teaching regarding taking oaths as found in Matthew 5:34-37?

Record the third commandment from Exodus 20:7.

What is the definition of the word "vain" in Exodus 20:7?

What do we learn about the importance of keeping an oath or promise if we make one?

a. Numbers 30:1-2

b. Deuteronomy 23:21-22

4. The purpose of the third commandment is to convince us that we can't keep our word. We can swear any kind of oath we want, but the weakness of our flesh never allows us to be truthful and honest. How did the scribes and Pharisees interpret the Law so that they could follow it?

What do we learn from Jesus' message to the scribes and Pharisees in Matthew 23:16-24?

What does James 5:12 teach us on this important matter?

There are times in the Bible and in our society where oath taking is both necessary and required. How does Hebrews 6:13, 14 illustrate the importance of God keeping His word in His promise to Abraham?

5. According to Matthew 5:38, what was Jesus' fifth example of the misuse of the Law by the scribes and Pharisees?

Read the Old Testament passages that are quoted here in Matthew 5.

a. Exodus 21:22-27

b. Deuteronomy 19:18-21

These are the Lord's instructions to the judges of the day concerning how to deal with criminals and offenses. They were to be a deterrent to crime, with punishment being appropriate and not oppressive. How did the Pharisees interpret the Law?

According to Matthew 5:39-42, what does Jesus say about the issue of retaliation, lawsuits, and personal mistreatment?

How did the Apostle Paul model Jesus' teaching in his response to Alexander, the coppersmith in 2Timothy 4:14?

Why is it important that we be sure to stay in context when interpreting the Scriptures?

In 1Peter 2:23, what example has our Lord Jesus given for us to follow?

What lies at the heart of the issue? Is it a matter of serving ourselves or serving Jesus by dying to ourselves?

Chapter 25
Illustration 6: Love Your Enemies
Matthew 5:43-48 (Luke 6:27-36)

Always begin every Bible Study with prayer. It is the Holy Spirit Who is your Teacher.

1. Read Matthew 5:43-48.

2. Read The Jesus Chronicles Chapter 25 (Pages 130-133).

3. For the sixth time, what was the popular teaching of the day as recorded in Matthew 5:43?

According to Leviticus 19:18, what was the actual teaching of the Law?

The Pharisees, who had no problem loving themselves, had completely altered God's command. Who would think that hating one's enemies would be a Bible verse? It's not! How is the word "hate" used in Psalm 139:21-22?

What did King David hate?

Jesus said, "You have heard it said...but I say..." What did He say in Matthew 5:44?

What is the definition of the word "love" in verse 44?

4. Jesus did not say, "Tolerate your enemies" or "don't kill your enemies". His command was to love them, bless them, do good to them, and pray for them. How do the following Scriptures support Jesus teaching and challenge you in your walk today?

a. Proverbs 25:21, 22

b. Romans 12:14

c. Romans 12:19-21

d. 1 Peter 3:8, 9

Religious people make up rules so they can satisfy their wicked hearts. Love your neighbor. Hate your enemy. This just makes good sense to the world. However, God requires His kids to live by a different standard, a higher standard. According to Matthew 5:45, why are we to behave so opposite of those in the world?

This higher standard of loving our enemy is only possible because Jesus Christ has given us a new nature, and we have the indwelling Holy Spirit to enable us to act in love in the face of our enemies. Our responsibility is to daily surrender our will to the control of the Holy Spirit. What more do we learn about this new nature?

a. Ezekiel 36:26, 27

b. Romans 13:12-14

c. 2Corinthians 3:17, 18

d. Colossians 3:9-11

5. As believers, we can have God's heart and His love. Things can change. The proof of this new birth is found in the doing of the impossible: in dying to self and loving our enemies. What do you read about the results of this new birth in John 13:34-35?

What further explanation does Jesus give us in Matthew 5:46-47 to prove that we are called to love in a far different manner than the world does?

Jesus finishes this topic by saying in Matthew 5:48, "Therefore you shall be perfect, just as your Father in heaven is perfect." How can this be?

What was His point to the Pharisees and to us?

How does Jesus' example from 1Peter 2:21-23 challenge and encourage you in your walk today?

Chapter 26
How and Why I Do What I Do
Matthew 6:1-4

Always begin every Bible Study with prayer. It is the Holy Spirit Who is your Teacher.

1. Read Matthew 6:1-4.

2. Read The Jesus Chronicles Chapter 26 (Pages 134-137).

3. In Matthew 6, the subject remains the same. What is that subject?

How does Jesus apply the lesson of the vast difference between works and grace in Matthew 6:1?

Jesus tells us that "religious" men are very interested in practicing their religion outwardly to be seen by others. How does the believer in Christ come to the Lord, and why?

What danger do we face as Christians when it comes to the long-term practice of our faith?

What is it that determines the acceptability of our faith?

How did the church of Ephesus in Revelation 2:1-5 "appear" to have it all together?

What had happened to them? What was the Lord's counsel?

4. The question in Matthew 6:1-4 is, "Why are you doing what you are doing?"

"Take heed" is a very solemn warning. There's a way to do things correctly, where the Lord receives honor, and the result of your spiritual life brings God glory. Read Luke 18:9-14.

Who was the parable spoken to?

What do you notice about the prayer of the Pharisee?

Whose prayer was heard that day? Why?

How does the lesson of Matthew 5:16 apply to our acts of giving to Jesus and to others?

5. According to Matthew 6:2-4, how are you, as a believer in Jesus, to give your gifts to the Lord?

What is the definition of a hypocrite?

Who is it the hypocritical doer of charitable deeds is trying to impress?

How did Cain exhibit this quality of hypocrisy?

What about the life of Judas? Did anyone expect he was the traitor?

It is not just about what we give, but how we give it! Read Mark 12:41-44. What do we learn from this amazing story about the heart of the true worshipper?

What do you think Jesus means by saying, "Don't let your left hand know what your right hand is doing?"

What is God looking for from you, as His child, when it comes to charitable deeds?

Chapter 27
Lessons on Prayer – Matthew 6:5-15
(Luke 11:2-4)

Always begin every Bible Study with prayer. It is the Holy Spirit Who is your Teacher.

1. Read Matthew 6:5-15.

2. Read The Jesus Chronicles Chapter 27 (Pages 138-147).

3. As Jesus distinguished between the religious practices of religious men and the faithful practices of believing saints, He spoke of motives for our behavior and of God's requirements. Jesus turns our attention to the practice of prayer. What instruction does He give us in Matthew 6:5-6?

What is the motive of the hypocrite when he comes to pray?

As a child of God, how and why should we seek Him in prayer?

The type of prayer God desires from us is one that focuses attention solely on Him. Too often we fall into the trap of hoping to impress others, or the opposite, being afraid to pray because we may not measure up. The prayer of the believer is to be a conversation with Jesus, plain and simple. Does Matthew 6:5,6 tell us that we should never pray in public?

What Biblical examples would you give to support your answer?

According to Matthew 6:7, how does the heathen fail in his doctrinal understanding of prayer?

Does it mean that we should not pray about something more than once?

If, as we learn in Matthew 6:8, your Father knows the things we have need of before we ask, why do we need to pray?

4. According to Luke, Jesus gave this outline that begins in Matthew 6:9 after His disciples had watched Him pray. He taught them in response to their request, "Lord, teach us to pray." Jesus gave them a concise sixty-four word outline on prayer recorded here in Matthew 6:9-13. Record the three parts of the outline:

Why is it important that our first petition toward God acknowledges Who we are praying to, and remember how we are related to Him?

What does it mean when Matthew 6:9 says, "Hallowed be Your name"?

With this second petition toward God in mind, what is to be the ultimate purpose of everything we pray and everything we say or do in our lives?

The third of the petitions toward God speaks of speaks of the Lord's rule over the earth. How does He, when will He, how is this already happening today?

Personal: These first three petitions are about relationship, worship, and surrender. Re-read Matthew 6:9-10 and use them as a guide to frame your prayer life today. Praying, "His kingdom come, His will be done," means your kingdom must go, and you must surrender to His will for your life...are you willing?

5. Once we have determined to let God be God, we can present our petitions before the Lord. According to Matthew 6:11-13a, what are the three areas of our lives we need to present to the Lord in prayer?

How often are we to seek the Lord in prayer for the needs in our lives?

God knows what we need before we ask. However, because we are by nature very independent, it is to our benefit to develop a dependence upon Him that is very real to us. As we seek the Lord for daily needs, our communication with Him reminds us to walk in obedience to His Word. What connection is made in Matthew 6:12 between the forgiveness we are granted and the forgiveness we extend to others?

This is the only portion of this outline of prayer that comes with further explanation. What are we told in Matthew 6:14-15? How will this truth affect how you forgive today?

Read Matthew 18:21-35. What does it teach you about the absolute necessity of walking in forgiveness?

What is the third petition for our personal needs found in Matthew 6:13a?

What did Jesus mean by "lead us not into temptation, but deliver us from the evil one?"

What is the reason God allows trials in our lives? How does the enemy seek to exploit those trials?

Finally, what is to be the concluding reminder in our prayer time according to Matthew 6:13b? How does it bring us full circle in prayer?

Chapter 28
Fasting: Food For Thought
Matthew 6:16-18

Always begin every Bible Study with prayer. It is the Holy Spirit Who is your Teacher.

1. Read Matthew 6:16-18.

2. Read The Jesus Chronicles Chapter 28 (Pages 148-151).

3. What was the third example Jesus used to illustrate the difference between the religious man and the believer?

How often was the nation of Israel required to fast according to the Law?

What requirements had they added, and how were many wrongly practicing the discipline of fasting?

What wrong motive was Jesus clearly addressing?

What is Jesus' instruction regarding fasting according to Matthew 6:16-18?

Did Jesus say that it was wrong to fast?

What phrase from Matthew 6:16 clearly tells us that, as believers in Jesus Christ, we should make it part of our spiritual habit to fast as the Lord leads?

4. There is no ordinary occasion in the Bible for fasting. Why is the believer to fast and under what four main types of circumstances?

1.

2.

3.

4.

Cite one Biblical example of the first, and most common, reason the believer is to practice the spiritual discipline of fasting.

How do the people's reactions to the government plan of annihilation in Esther 4:1-3 illustrate the second reason for fasting?

Read 2Chronicles 20:1-3. What action did King Jehoshaphat take in the face of a tremendous enemy army?

What is the third reason you will find in the Bible for seeking the Lord in fasting? Give an example of when we see this type of fast taking place.

Finally, what is the fourth reason that believers are called to fast and pray? When do we see this type of fast in the lives of godly men and women in the Bible?

5. Isaiah 58 is the definitive chapter on the subject of fasting. Read Isaiah 58 and explain how the people practiced fasting.

How does Isaiah describe the type of fast that pleases the Lord?

From Isaiah 58:6, 7, list the promised outcome of the fast when it is led by the Lord and practiced by a believer whose heart is truly surrendered to Jesus.

1.

2.

3.

4.

5.

6.

What is the promised outcome of the Spirit led fast as given to us in Isaiah 58:8, 9?

Personal: Have you considered the spiritual discipline of fasting? Jesus expected us to fast...He said, "When you fast..." Will you seek His heart on this issue in your walk with Jesus? There's a lot to be gained by seeking Him!

Chapter 29
Your Treasure and Your Master
Matthew 6:19-24

Always begin every Bible Study with prayer. It is the Holy Spirit Who is your Teacher.

1. Read Matthew 6:19-24.

2. Read The Jesus Chronicles Chapter 29 (Pages 152-156).

3. Beginning in verse 19, the topic of Jesus' teaching changed from private devotion to public life as He gave His disciples some examples of how their relationship with Him should affect the way they were living. A relationship with Jesus ought to be seen. It ought to be measurable. It ought to change lives. According to Matthew 6:19, 20, what radical command did Jesus give to the believer regarding the acquisition of treasure?

How would you define the word "treasures" in verses 19-20?

What does it mean when we are commanded to "lay up" treasures in heaven?

What instruction are we given in the following Scriptures about how to handle the material gifts we receive from the Lord?

a. Psalm 62:10

b. Proverbs 23:4, 5

c. Hebrews 13:5

d. 1John 2:15, 16

What does 1Peter 1:3-5 teach us about the treasure that is laid up for us in heaven?

Does this command prohibit hard work and success in this world? Explain your answer.

4. Laying up treasure in heaven is a matter of where your values lie. What does Matthew 6:21 teach us about the attachment between where we store our treasure and where we invest our heart?

Practically speaking, how can you deposit your treasures in heaven?

What critical lesson do we learn from the warning and the parable of Luke 12:15 – 21?

What are we to take heed of?

What do we learn about the things that are truly valuable in this life?

How does Hebrews 11:13-16 help you to maintain a proper view of this short life we live and the reason we live?

Personal: Where are you storing your treasure? What needs to change? Will you ask the Lord to help you make the needed changes?

5. The Bible clearly teaches us that our heart is singular in its ability to focus and it can only be completely occupied with one thing at a time. How does Matthew 6:22 and 23 illustrate this truth?

If your eye is on the things of God, focused on God's will and on eternity, you will be single-minded and full of light. What do we learn about this light that must fully inhabit our heart and life?

a. Psalm 119:105

b. Matthew 5:16

c. John 1:1-4

d. 2Corinthians 4:6

e. Revelation 21:23

Mammon is literally the god of wealth. What definitive conclusion is made in Matthew 6:24? Do you truly believe it?

Review the comparison list on page 156 in The Jesus Chronicles. Where is your treasure? Who is your master? You can't serve both! You have to decide. The sooner the better!

Chapter 30
Why I Don't Have To Worry – Matthew 6:25-34
(Luke 12:22-31)

Always begin every Bible Study with prayer. It is the Holy Spirit Who is your Teacher.

1. Read Matthew 6:25-34.

2. Read The Jesus Chronicles Chapter 30 (Pages 157-161).

3. In these ten verses, Jesus focuses on the essentials of life – eating, drinking, and clothing – the things we can't do without. If you were going to summarize these ten verses, what would you say?

   In case you have a hard time narrowing the lesson down, read Matthew 6:25, 6:31, and 6:34. What is the lesson?

   What four important lessons do we learn from Jesus' teaching to His disciples on the subject of worry?

   1.

   2.

   3.

   4.

   When Jesus says in Matthew 6:25, "do not worry about your life", what part of your life is He speaking about?

   Why is worry a sin against the Lord?

What is the definition of the word "worry" found in Matthew 6:25?

Personal: Have you ever felt strangled by worry?

What is the origin of this sin of worry?

3. What do we learn about the characteristic of contentment that ought to dominate the life of the believer?

   a. Philippians 4:11-13

   b. 1 Timothy 6:6-8

   c. Hebrew 13:5-6

Whether you have to live from meal to meal, or paycheck to paycheck, or your refrigerator and bank account have abundant provision, the lesson Jesus is teaching remains the same. It is still crucial that we understand it today. What common examples from nature does Jesus refer to in Matthew 6:26-30?

What does the word "stature" in Matthew 6:27 refer to?

Personal: Will you determine to trust Jesus regarding the things in your life that you have not been dealing with in faith, fully trusting God's sovereign care for you?

4. Our Heavenly Father feeds the birds and clothes the hillsides with flowers more beautiful than a king's garments. How much more will He meet the needs of His sons and daughters! Can you add a day to your life by worrying? How does Jesus describe the follower who is always strangled by worry in verse 30?

What do we learn from the following accounts where Jesus instructed His followers who had "little faith"?

a. Matthew 8:23-27

b. Matthew 14:28-33

c. Matthew 16:6-12

Worry is not a trivial sin to God because it says, "I don't believe You and I don't trust You." God's ultimate for you is that you would rest in the contentment of His provision without worry or fear. What contrast is drawn in Matthew 6:31, 32 between the life of the true believer and those in the world?

What is the solution to our problem of worrying according to Matthew 6:33 and 34?

How do the following Scriptures encourage you to trust the Lord for your needs?

a. Psalm 37:23-25

b. Psalm 84:11,12

c. Philippians 4:19

Chapter 31
Jesus on Judging – Matthew 7:1-12
(Luke 6:37-42)

Always begin every Bible Study with prayer. It is the Holy Spirit Who is your Teacher.

1. Read Matthew 7:1-12.

2. Read The Jesus Chronicles Chapter 31 (Pages 162-166).

3. Here in Matthew 7, Jesus addresses two issues as He continues setting the religious man beside the saved man. What two issues are discussed in Matthew 7:1-12?

   What command is given to us in Matthew 7:1?

   What does Jesus mean by the instruction, "Judge not"?

   How do you explain this command in light of the discussion of church discipline and inter-personal relationships discussed in Matthew 18:15-20?

   If you followed these steps of church order, would you be required to pass some type of judgment?

   What type of judgment is spoken of in 2John 1:9-11?

Why can the need for judgment in the above example co-exist with the command of Matthew 7:1?

What type of judgment does God never allow us to participate in?

4. Judgment is like a boomerang. You throw it out, and it comes right back to you. What sobering warning is given to us in Matthew 7:2?

What do we learn from James 2:13?

What do we learn from Matthew 7:3-5 about the inherent dangers of thinking we know the hearts and minds of others?

Not only do we have a poor view of others, but also we have a poor view of ourselves; though for ourselves we make many concessions and come with great patience. Why does our sin look so much worse in someone else's life?

How did the Lord reveal the sin of King David through the prophet Nathan?

According to 2Samuel 12:1-7, what judgment did David declare for the sinner who stole and slaughtered his neighbor's only lamb?

5. What instruction is given to us in Matthew 7:6 that tells us that there is a time when we have told the unbeliever all we know to no avail?

Does this require you to make a judgment about the person with whom you have been sharing the Word? Do you, or can you, know their eternal state or destiny?

How does the topic of prayerful fellowship with God apply to this discussion of judging and not judging?

What instruction is given in Matthew 7:7-11?

In the end, regardless of how we are treated, we are to love others not to the degree that they love us, but to the degree we would like to be loved by them, and as we learn here in the Gospels, as Jesus loved us. How then should we treat others according to Matthew 7:12?

What instruction are we given in Romans 13:8 & 10 that is an excellent guide when trying to boldly share the Gospel with our friends and neighbors?

Chapter 32
How Do I Get To Heaven From Here?
Matthew 7:13-14 (Luke 13:24)

Always begin every Bible Study with prayer. It is the Holy Spirit Who is your Teacher.

1. Read Matthew 7:13-14.

2. Read The Jesus Chronicles Chapter 32 (Pages 167-171).

3. We have come to the final point Jesus made in this sermon that He taught to the apostles. Beginning in Matthew 5 He taught on the subjects of praying, giving, fasting, storing up treasures, passing judgment, and worrying. He set the concerns of the religious person alongside the life of the believer. He concluded with a call for decision, "What path will you choose?" How does Matthew 7:13-14 describe the two choices?

Why do you think Jesus described the road to heaven as being through the narrow gate?

What do we learn about this narrow gate from the following Scriptures?

a. Luke 13:24-25

b. Luke 14:26-33

c. John 10:9-11

d. John 14:6

e. Acts 4:12

4. We are required to make many decisions each day and major ones throughout our lifetime - only one decision has eternal consequences. After three chapters of instruction, Jesus tied it all together and said, "Come and follow Me." Yet in keeping with God's sovereign will, He always has allowed people to make their own decision. What do you learn about this required choice from the following Biblical accounts?

a. Deuteronomy 30:19-20

b. Joshua 24:15

c. 1 Kings 18:21

In Matthew 7:13-14 Jesus clearly laid out a simple choice. The choice is between the many false ways to God and the one true way Jesus offered. There have always been only two systems of religion. After such detailed study of the beatitudes, how would you describe these two paths?

From here through the end of chapter 7 Jesus gives multiple illustrations that there are two ways: man's or God's. How does the word enter speak to the issue of the need for a choice?

5. The Gospel's message is narrow because Jesus made it that way. It's a small passage. It allows for only one-way: faith in Him, rather than works and faith in them. How does Paul clearly state this narrow path in 1 Timothy 2:3-6?

There are not only two gates, but these gates lead to two ways: one that is broad and other that is difficult. Obviously the broad way is more popular – in fact – what popular terms are used repeatedly in media and social discussion to promote the advantages of the broad way?

We are also told in Matthew 7:13-14 that these two gates and their two paths lead to two destinations. What are they?

Finally, we read of two groups. The Lord distinguished them by the words "many" and "few". The broad road has the most travelers – the majority – the "in crowd". At the end, many will claim to be followers of Jesus but will be shocked. How does Matthew 7:22, 23 describe the Lord's response to their claims?

Does the narrow gate or the difficult road mean that all are not invited, welcomed, or sought after?

How do the following invitations support your answer, and how might you be able to use them to share with someone who feels God would not call them to Himself?

a. Isaiah 55:1-7

b. Jeremiah 29:11-14

c. John 3:14-18

Chapter 33
Beware of False Prophets – Matthew 7:15-20
(Luke 6:43-45)

Always begin every Bible Study with prayer. It is the Holy Spirit Who is your Teacher.

1. Read Matthew 7:15-20.

2. Read The Jesus Chronicles Chapter 33 (Pages 172-175).

3. As Jesus sat down with His disciples and gave them this first sermon, He talked about the difference between God's way of life and ours, God's way of salvation, and everything else, and faith in Him versus self-accomplishment. What warning are we given in Matthew 7:15 about the danger and difficulty that we are sure to encounter even when we have chosen the narrow path?

According to the account of Adam and Eve in Genesis 3:1-5, whose message fills the heart of the false prophet?

According to Genesis 3:1, what was the serpent's objective as he questioned Eve about God's instructions and commands?

The false prophets always challenge God, His Word and His love as they seek to promote themselves and their agenda. What warning did Moses give to Joshua, as he was about to lead the children of Israel into the Promised Land?

From Isaiah 30:8-11, what do we learn about the heart of the person who wants only good news from the prophet rather than the truth?

What more do we learn about the false prophet, his methods, his motives and his fruit?

a. Romans 16:17, 18

b. 1 Timothy 4:1, 2

c. 2 John 1:7

d. Acts 20:29, 30

4. There's a large market in the world today for the false prophet and his message. As in the days of Isaiah, many only want to hear what will make them feel better, not what will heal them for good. What were the two things that distinguished the true prophet of God in the Old Testament?

What did the Lord say to His people in Jeremiah 5:31 about the false prophets? What is the definition of the word "beware" in Matthew 7:15?

The false prophets are more than wrong; they're dangerous to your spiritual well being. The wolves are the common enemy of the sheep. What adjective does Jesus use to illustrate the severe danger of these false prophets?

Therefore, we are to "beware", "take heed", and "be on guard", because the false prophet is not impersonating a sheep, he is disguising himself as a shepherd. He is often most identifiable by what he does not say. According to Matthew 7:16-20, how will we be able to know the truth about the motives of those who seek to lead?

5. It is our responsibility as believers to evaluate the fruit in the lives of the teachers and preachers from whom we receive our Biblical teaching. This does not mean we are judgmental, critical, or negative. It simply means that we are to check fruit. What did Paul say about the Bereans in Acts 17:11, and how will you be able to follow their example in your walk today?

As you go through your Bible, you will see at least three "C's" of fruit inspection that make the truth known to all who follow. What are they, and how will they reveal the truth in the heart of the teacher?

1.

2.

3.

Record the warning from Matthew 7:15.

We have learned that there are two gates, two roads, and two types of teachers. How can we be certain that we will not be deceived by the false doctrine of false prophets?

a. 2Timothy 2:15

b. 2Timothy 3:16, 17

c. Hebrews 4:12

Chapter 34
Saying, Hearing, and Doing – Matthew 7:21-29
(Luke 6:46-49)

Always begin every Bible Study with prayer. It is the Holy Spirit Who is your Teacher.

1. Read Matthew 7:21-29.

2. Read The Jesus Chronicles Chapter 34 (Pages 176-179).

3. After three chapters of differentiation between faith and works, between God's grace and people's efforts, between the broad way and the narrow road, Jesus concludes this first sermon with two illustrations. What point does He make that has eternal consequences?

Jesus turns from the subject of unsound teachers to that of unsound hearers because not only can false prophets deceive us, we can deceive ourselves. What do we learn about hearing and doing from James 1:22-25?

It is human nature to look at ourselves with a bias. What do we learn about the difference between someone who truly knows Jesus and someone who merely agrees with Him but doesn't follow Him?

Matthew 7:21 tells us, "Not everyone who says to Me, 'Lord, Lord' shall enter the kingdom of heaven." Who will?

What do we learn from Matthew 25:1-13 about the importance of having the right relationship to Jesus?

4. In even the weakest of saints there is a desire to be more like Jesus, a hatred of the sin in their own lives, and a desire for God's Spirit to work in and through them. How does Jesus describe those He tells to depart from Him?

What does Luke 6:46 add to your understanding about those who say, "Lord, Lord"?

In the illustration in Matthew 7:21-23 we are told that those whom the Lord did not know had done some amazing works. How did they accomplish these?

A profession of faith and a practice of lawlessness are not compatible. If you get saved, it shows. Go back and read Matthew 7:17-20 from Chapter 33. How will you know if someone is truly saved?

What more do you learn from the following Scriptures about obedience and lawlessness?

a. 1Samuel 15:22

b. Psalm 51:16, 17

c. Micah 6:6-8

5. Read Matthew 7:24-29. What are the differences between these two builders and their two houses?

What happens when the storm of life comes that reveals the true nature of the building (the faith)?

How do the following verses help you evaluate the foundation on which you have built your life?

a. John 14:15

b. John 15:10

c. 1 John 2:3, 4

d. 1 John 5:2, 3

If you want to be sure you are saved, do what God says. People who obey God from a true heart do so not because someone else is pressuring them to do so. They obey Him because He is at work in their lives. What recent evidence have you seen of Jesus transforming your heart and life?

Personal: Are you sure your faith is built on the solid rock of Jesus? Don't wait until it is too late!

Chapter 35
Who's the Boss? – Luke 7:1-10
(Matthew 8:5-13)

Always begin every Bible Study with prayer. It is the Holy Spirit Who is your Teacher.

1. Read Luke 7:1-10.

2. Read The Jesus Chronicles Chapter 35 (Pages 180-184).

3. Following Jesus' three-chapter sermon of the difference between the religious man and the man of faith, we come to the account that Matthew and Luke give about His arrival in Capernaum. What do we learn about this city on the Sea of Galilee?

   What was the tragic circumstance faced the centurion in Capernaum?

   What did the Jewish elders of Capernaum observe about this centurion?

   Was their opinion based upon his works or his relationship with God?

   Jesus had just finished saying, "If you'll build your house on the rock, your house will stand." Yet immediately, here comes the religious thinking heaven can be had for a price. Paul tried to serve God in this manner, but when he met Jesus all things changed. What does Paul tell us in Philippians 3:4-9 that clearly defines the difference between works and faith?

The elders of the day related to the Lord solely on the basis of merit, performance, and goodness. Most people still do. However, it is not to be so in the church. Do you ever find yourself trying to earn God's love or approval?

4. According to Luke 7:6-7, what was the centurion's opinion of himself?

How did the opinions of the elders differ from this man's self-examination?

How does Luke 7:8 explain the attitude with which the centurion approached Jesus?

What do we learn from the following Scriptures about how we are to seek the Lord?

a. Psalm 25:9

b. Matthew 5:5

c. James 1:21

5. We have heard what the Jewish elders thought of this centurion and what he thought of himself. According to Luke 7:9-10, what is the opinion of the One Who matters most?

What was the Roman centurion declaring about Jesus' authority?

What do we learn about the absolute authority of Jesus Christ?

a. Isaiah 9:6, 7

b. John 5:24-27

c. Philippians 2:9-11

d. Colossians 1:16-19

Gideon had 32,000 men to fight the Midianites. It was far too many for him to learn that it was God Who brings the victory. The LORD sent him into battle with 300 men. The victory was theirs. God received the glory. Jesus does have all authority. Is there something in your life that you haven't fully trusted Him for? Will you surrender it to Him today?

Record Jeremiah 32:27. Do you truly believe it is true?

Chapter 36
The Widow of Nain Meets the Lord
Luke 7:11-17

Always begin every Bible Study with prayer. It is the Holy Spirit Who is your Teacher.

1. Read Luke 7:11-17.

2. Read The Jesus Chronicles Chapter 36 (Pages 185-190).

3. This story takes place the day after the centurion's servant was healed. Who initiated this interaction?

Luke writes this story and calls us to "pay particular attention" to the details. Imagine being there to witness this meeting of two crowds. What might you have seen, heard, and felt?

The word "behold" calls us to examine the details. It is used frequently in the New Testament. What important details are we to observe and understand from the following Scriptures?

a. Matthew 1:23

b. Matthew 2:1-12

c. Matthew 17:1-5

d. Matthew 28:1-7

4. What is the lesson in Luke 7:11-12 that speaks of God's timing and sovereignty?

Choose one of the Biblical accounts discussed on pages 186-187 in the Jesus Chronicles. Read the account and explain how it encourages you when you feel God's timing does not align with your desire or plans.

At the gates of Nain, the excited and enthusiastic crowd collides with the funeral procession for a widow's only son. What does Luke 7:13 tell us about the Lord's heart toward the broken-hearted woman?

What do we learn about our Lord's understanding and compassion regarding circumstances and tragedies in our lives?

a. Hebrews 2:17, 18

b. Hebrews 4:13-16

c. Isaiah 63:8, 9

5. What does Jesus say to the widow of Nain?

Why is it that He is the only one who could make such an unusual request at a funeral?

What are some other Biblical commands given to us that run counter to common sense and the world's values?

Jesus stopped the procession, and though He was not asked to help, with love as His motivation and as God come in the flesh, He said to the woman, "Don't weep." According to Luke 7:14, what did He say to the young man?

What happened?

What was the response to the crowd of onlookers?

In Nain, Jesus, saw the result of sin and presented Himself as the One in whom we can find victory over death. He brings life. What do we learn regarding Jesus' power from His own words in Luke 7:20-23?

Read the prophecy of Zacharias at the birth of John the Baptist in Luke 1:67-79. How do these words encourage you today as you walk with Jesus? Will you trust His promise and heed His direction? Since He is God, it would be unreasonable to do anything else.

Chapter 37
Doubt and the Believer – Luke 7:18-23
(Matthew 11:2-6)

Always begin every Bible Study with prayer. It is the Holy Spirit Who is your Teacher.

1. Read Luke 7:18-23.

2. Read The Jesus Chronicles Chapter 37 (Pages 191-196).

3. In Luke 7:17 we read that the amazing news of the miracles Jesus performed had spread 80 miles south to Judea and all the way to the Dead Sea where John the Baptist was imprisoned. Why was John in jail?

How long had he been there?

Who did John send to Jesus, and what was their question?

What event took place in Matthew 3:13-17 that would have caused John to know and trust in Jesus?

Can you understand why John may have begun to have doubts?

What did you learn about God's heart toward those who have doubts and are truly seeking answers?

4. The reports John was hearing about what Jesus was doing didn't line up with what he was looking for, because his understanding – like that of most people in the first century – was that when the Messiah came He would be a political deliverer. So doubt began to rise in his heart. When God seems inactive, we tend to doubt. What is the difference between honest doubt and stubborn unbelief?

How is Abraham's life an example of both honest doubt and deliberate disobedience?

Read Judges 6:33 – 40. The Lord met Gideon's doubt by showing him miracles involving the fleece of wool.
Even though God answered him to strengthen his faith, do you think He would have rather had Gideon trust Him without needing this proof?

You read of the doubts of Martha, Thomas, and the church in Acts. How has the lesson helped you to walk in more faith and trust today?

What do you learn from the following Scriptures about our need to walk in trust?

a. Psalm 37:3-5

b. Proverbs 3:5, 6

c. Isaiah 26:3

d. Jeremiah 17:7, 8

5. God blesses those who honestly struggle to grow because He wants us to know Him. The whole question and answer process establishes our trust in God, gives us an answer for the hope that lies within us, and pushes us to find out what's true and what's not. What is the common cause of most doubt in our lives?

When we find ourselves slipping into doubt, what is one solution?

According to Luke 7:20-22, what was Jesus' answer to the two disciples John sent to Him?

How do we see the emphasis on Jesus' work supported by His word in these verses?

a. John 5: 36, 37

b. John 14:9-11

Paul wondered "why" God allowed him to suffer. What was the Lord's response to his question in 2Corinthians 12:9-10?

What encouragement are we given in Luke 7:23 to remind us that when our expectations of what we think God is or should be don't align themselves with God's Word, we must trust His Word and not stumble?

Chapter 38
Jesus Speaks of the Faithful
and the Not So Faithful
Luke 7:24-35 - (Matthew 11:7-19)

Always begin every Bible Study with prayer. It is the Holy Spirit Who is your Teacher.

1. Read Luke 7:24-35.

2. Read The Jesus Chronicles Chapter 38 (Pages 197-201).

3. After John's disciples left, Jesus turned to the crowds that remained. According to Luke 7:24-26, what question did He pose to them?

Read Matthew 3:1-12. What do we learn about John the Baptist's message and his ministry?

Who came to see him and why?

Jesus defended John in very glowing terms. Even though John had momentary questions of doubt, his message was strong, powerful and unwavering. Jesus quotes a prophecy from Malachi 3:1 regarding John. What does it tell us about John the Baptist?

What does Luke 7:28 tell us about John's status amongst the prophets?

There are two reasons that he held this most important status. What are they?

4. When Jesus spoke to the people about John in Matthew 11:14, to whom did He compare him and why?

Was he Elijah?

How was he like Elijah?

The Lord allowed John a place of honor as point man of great privilege. He preached one message. What was it?

What did Jesus mean when He said in Luke 7:28, "but he who is least in the kingdom of God is greater than he?"

Why does the believer in Jesus Christ have a greater privilege, a greater position, and a greater message than John the Baptist?

How will truth change your perspective and your actions today?

5. Hearing Jesus' testimony thrilled many of the people's hearts. They agreed with John that they were sinful and needed help and that the Messiah was soon to come. Sadly, amongst them there was also the religious group who refused the message and denied their need. According to Luke 7:30, what they were rejecting?

What do we learn from 1 Timothy 2:3-6 about the heart and the desire of the Lord toward mankind?

The Gospel requires a choice in each person's life. It is not possible to walk the fence, to play both sides, or be undecided. What clear decision is called for in Joshua 24:15?

What was Elijah's direction to God's people in 1 Kings 18:21?

Jesus used an illustration to speak to the heart of the scribes' and Pharisees' rejection of both John's message and His own message. Read Luke 7:31-35. What is He teaching us about the hardened hearts of some who hear the Gospel?

We are told that wisdom is known of her children. What is the difference between childlikeness and childishness?

John the Baptist called for self-evaluation and confession of sin. Jesus offers grace and mercy through faith. The wise will respond. The foolish will not. As His followers, what is our responsibility when it comes to sharing the Gospel?

What promise do we find in Isaiah 55:11 that ought to emboldened us to share Jesus with those we meet today?

Some will answer God's call and come to Him. Others will reject the invitation. It is our ministry to tell the world that Jesus is the only answer. What does Paul teach us in 1Corinthians 1:17, 18 about the message of the cross?

Chapter 39
Jesus Loves Sinners
Luke 7:36-50

Always begin every Bible Study with prayer. It is the Holy Spirit Who is your Teacher.

1. Read Luke 7:36-50.

2. Read The Jesus Chronicles Chapter 39 (Pages 202-207).

3. In Matthew 11, we come to a discussion Jesus had with the crowd just before He went to the Pharisee's house for dinner. What was Jesus' message in Matthew 11:20-24, and how did it apply to these hardhearted listeners?

In prayer, what tender invitation does Jesus extend in Matthew 11:25-30?

How might His prayer have convinced this broken woman that even she could boldly seek Him?

Re-read Matthew 11:28-30. How does this invitation speak to your heart today?

What promises are you given in this invitation?

What instructions must you follow and practice in your daily walk with Jesus?

4. The chronology now shifts from the discussion and prayer in Matthew 11 to Luke 7 and a woman who is drawn to seek Jesus. Imagine her hearing that He would welcome even a sinner like her if she humbly came to Him. On the contrary, what was the motive of the Pharisee who invited Jesus to dinner?

Describe the interaction from Luke 7:37-39 that occurred as this woman, whose life was shattered, meets her Savior.

In contrast, what were the "thoughts" of the Pharisee as he watched Jesus deal with the woman who washed Jesus feet?

What analogy did Jesus make in Luke 7:41-43 to explain the intense love of this repentant woman and why others are far less devoted to the Lord?

What three common courtesies were not extended to Jesus as He entered the Pharisees house?

What does the Bible teach us about the sinful state of all of mankind?

a. Romans 3:23

b. 1John 1:8-10

5. The issue for Simon was that he didn't see himself very deeply in debt. However, what clear and concise truth is given to us in Romans 6:23a?

Does it say just the worst of the worst sinner deserves death?

Who deserves death?

What great news is given to us in Romans 6:23b?

Why do you think it is harder to reach the "fifty denarii" sinner with the truth of the Gospel than it is to reach the "five hundred denarii" one?

Personal: Do you realize that you are deeply indebted to Jesus? It doesn't matter where your life has taken you; Jesus is offering life eternal and forgiveness of each and every sin. Write a prayer of thanksgiving for the new life He has given you!

As Jesus turned to the woman, He continued to talk to Simon. How does Luke 7:47 explain the intense love this woman had for Jesus that drew her into the den of religious haters to find Him?

Not only did she realize her sins were many, she realized God could forgive them all. Write out Jesus' instructions to this woman from Luke 7:50.

Is this the truth in which you fully place your faith? If not, you can do so today, and then "Go in peace."

Chapter 40
The Unpardonable Sin – Mark 3:20-35
(Matthew 12:31-32; Luke 11:14-21)

Always begin every Bible Study with prayer. It is the Holy Spirit Who is your Teacher.

1. Read Mark 3:20-35.

2. Read The Jesus Chronicles Chapter 40 (Pages 208-212).

3. In Mark 3, Jesus returned to Peter's house in Capernaum. What does Mark 3:20 tells us about the intensity of ministry on this day?

The crowds just kept coming. They pressed in, again and again. It wasn't an isolated event! What was the response of Jesus' family to His ministry?

What does John 7:3-10 show us about the attitude of Jesus' brothers toward His ministry?

Have you ever had anyone declare you to be "crazy" because of your devotion to Jesus? What do you learn from this account in Mark that helps you to understand the reaction of those who are not following Jesus?

Jesus' family thought He had lost His mind. The crowd's view was that they needed Him daily, day and night. What did the scribes and Pharisees claim about Him?

4. Matthew 12:22 gives us the context of this comment by the Scribes and Pharisees. Who was brought to Jesus, and what did He do for him?

Matthew tells us in chapter 12:25 that Jesus knew the thoughts of the men who were attributing His power to the Devil. According to Mark 3:23-27, what was Jesus response to their accusations?

No one can enter into a strong man's house and rob him unless he first is able to bind the strong man. Who is the strong man in Jesus' parable, and what is the house?

What do we learn about the power of the enemy and our deliverance in Jesus Christ?

a. 1John 3:8, 9

b. 1John 5:19, 20

5. Jesus' logic left the Pharisees speechless. Jesus wanted to be sure the men who accused Him of being in league with the Devil understood that there would be grave consequences for maintaining their position. What strong statement does Jesus make in Mark 3:28-30?

In as few words as possible, define the sin of blasphemy against the Holy Spirit.

How does the life of Pharaoh, in the days of his interaction with Moses, illustrate the sin of blasphemy of the Holy Spirit?

What warning are we given in Genesis 6:3?

When Jesus' family arrived in Capernaum from twenty-five miles away in Nazareth, the crowd was so large they couldn't get inside to see Him. According to Mark 3:31-35, what was Jesus' response to their message?

Compare Jesus' response to Mark 3:21. How does His reaction illustrate that He understood what they thought of Him?

Who is Jesus' family?

a. John 1:9-13

b. Romans 8:14-16

c. 2Corinthians 6:17, 18

The choice is yours, and it is an individual choice! Who do you think Jesus is? Is He a lunatic, a demonically driven liar, or the King of kings and the Lord of lords? If you haven't answered the call of the Holy Spirit, do so today – don't wait too long.

Chapter 41
How Do You Hear – Luke 8:1-15
(Matthew 13:1-23; Mark 4:1-20)

Always begin every Bible Study with prayer. It is the Holy Spirit Who is your Teacher.

1. Read Luke 8:1-15.

2. Read The Jesus Chronicles Chapter 41 (Pages 213-217).

3. In Luke 8:1-3 we are given a general statement about Jesus' Galilean ministry. Where was Jesus traveling and what was His message?

Who was traveling with Him?

Why would they leave everything behind to follow and serve the Lord?

What important lesson do we learn from the life of Mary of Magdala?

As the Lord ministers to you, why do you give to Him and serve Him?

4. Read Luke 8:4-10. Who was in this multitude that was following Jesus?

What style of teaching does Jesus use amongst this crowd?

How would you define a parable?

Why did Jesus teach in parables?

In the four verses of Luke 8:5-8, we have the parable of the sower; it is vitally important that we correctly interpret its meaning. What does the term "expositional constancy" mean, and how does it apply to this parable?

Jesus clearly explained this parable to the disciples, and it is the standard by which we can interpret all other parables. According to Luke 8:11, what does the seed represent?

The seed is the Word of God. What more do we learn about the Word of God?

a. Romans 10:17

b. Ephesians 6:17

c. Hebrews 4:12

d. Hebrews 11:3

e. 1 Peter 1:23-24

5. What happened to the following seeds, and why?

Fell by the wayside:

Fell upon the rocks:

Fell among the thorns:

Who stole away the seed that landed by the wayside?

What is the difference between an emotional response to the Word of God and true repentance?

When the seed fell among the thorns, what three things can choke out God's Word?

We see that there are hard-hearted, shallow-hearted, and emotional responders that do not retain God's Word in their hearts. Fortunately, there are also willing hearts. What does Luke 8:15 say about the seed that fell on good ground?

What lesson do we learn from this parable that will help as we determine to spread the seed of God's Word to those around us who do not yet know Jesus?

Chapter 42
He Spoke To Them in Parables
Matthew 13:10-17, 24-52

Always begin every Bible Study with prayer. It is the Holy Spirit Who is your Teacher.

1. Read Matthew 13:10-17, 24-52.

2. Read The Jesus Chronicles Chapter 42 (Pages 218-223).

3. Excluding the parable of the sower covered in Chapter 41, in Matthew 13 we find six parables Jesus shared with the crowds and His disciples. What two-fold reason did He give for using parables as a means of teaching?

Why would Jesus seek to hide the truth from those who would not respond?

How are parables beneficial to those who are truly seeking to learn spiritual truth?

What is the topic of all six of the parables we are studying in this text?

What statement is being made through all these parables?

Read Matthew 13:24-30 & 36-43.

Who is the One who sows the good seed?

What is the field?

Who are the good seeds?

Who are the tares?

Who is the enemy who sowed the tares?

When will the harvest take place?

Who are the reapers?

What lesson about the apparent size of the church will help you in your walk with Jesus today?

4. Read Matthew 13:31-32. To reinforce the lesson, Jesus told another parable about a mustard seed that became a tree. This is an often-misinterpreted parable. The picture here is of something that looks bigger than it actually is. What do the birds represent?

What warning is found in Matthew 7:21-23 regarding those who look and act like believers but are not?

In the third parable (Matthew 13:33), Jesus speaks about leaven. What is it? How does it affect the church?

What lesson does this parable give us about how the enemy works within the church?

What concern did Paul have as he wrote to the church at Corinth in 2Corinthians 11:3-4 regarding the introduction of false teaching in the church?

What warning is found in the following verses that when heeded will protect you from being led astray?

a. 2Corinthians 11:13-15

b. 2Peter 2:1-2

c. 1John 4:1-3

5. According to Matthew 13:36, the parables Jesus gave to the disciples apart from the crowds actually begin in verse 44. Why would it be so important that these future church leaders would understand God's heart toward the lost?

What is the kingdom of heaven "like" according to the following Scripture references?

a. Matthew 13:44

b. Matthew 13:45-46

c. Matthew 13:47-50

The Lord gave these six parables to His disciples, against a backdrop of several thousand people clamoring for His attention, because He saw the success of His work very differently than they did. We each need to answer the question for ourselves. Are you "in" or "out"? Are you "of" or "not of"?

God would have us see that the true church is smaller than the claimed church, and for those who answer His invitation, He willfully and gladly gave all to save us. What is your job now? What is not?

Chapter 43
A Late-Night Boat Ride – Mark 4:35-41
(Matthew 8:23-27; Luke 8:22-25)

Always begin every Bible Study with prayer. It is the Holy Spirit Who is your Teacher.

1. Read Mark 4:35-41.

2. Read The Jesus Chronicles Chapter 43 (Pages 224-228).

3. The day had begun in Capernaum at Peter's house, and the ministry continued all day. Jesus healed the man who had been possessed by the devil and was blind and mute. According to Mark 4:35-38, what was Jesus' plan when evening had come?

What were Jesus' precise instructions to the disciples regarding their crossing of the sea?

What lesson can we learn from watching the disciples panic while Jesus slept?

How can you specifically apply this lesson to the storms in your life?

Sometimes we come to the conclusion that if we are facing storms or trials, we are not in God's will. How does this account of the storm speak to this wrong conclusion?

When these seasoned fishermen were at the end of their expertise, what did they do? (Mark 4:38)

Why did they wait so long?

How does Proverbs 3:5, 6 speak to this issue we often deal with?

4. The disciples found themselves in a position where their expertise at handling storms in a boat was overwhelmed by the intensity of the storm itself. They had nowhere else to turn. According to Mark 4:38-39, what action did they take?

What absolute wrong assumption did the disciples make as they woke Jesus?

How is this assumption proven wrong in God's Word?

a. Deuteronomy 31:6-8

b. 1Samuel 12:22

c. Isaiah 49:14-16

d. Hebrews 13:5

The lesson we need to learn is that unexpected storms are not out of God's hand. Just because He doesn't do something right away doesn't mean He isn't in charge. How do the following Scriptures support this truth?

a. Romans 8:28

b. 2Corinthians 4:15-17

c. 1Peter 1:6-8

5. What did Jesus do, according to Mark 4:39-41, when the disciples woke Jesus from His nap?

What was the disciples' response?

Read Matthew 8:23-27. What question did Jesus ask the disciples?

Personal: Have you ever heard Him whisper this in your ear?

What do you learn from this account of the disciples in the storm that will help you to overcome fear of the unknown and unexpected circumstances in your life?

Listen carefully – because how you hear is as important as what you hear. Record Luke 8:18, and add a prayer of willingness to trust Jesus in the midst of your storm.

Chapter 44
Man of the Tombs – Luke 8:26-39
(Matthew 8:28-34; Mark 5:1-20)

Always begin every Bible Study with prayer. It is the Holy Spirit Who is your Teacher.

1. Read Luke 8:26-39.

2. Read The Jesus Chronicles Chapter 44 (Pages 229-234).

3. This account of the man of the tombs is found in all of the synoptic Gospels – Matthew, Mark, and Luke. What does it tell us about the character of the Devil and his will to seek our destruction?

How long had this man of the tombs been tormented, and what were his living conditions like?

What is the primary means by which the enemy does his work in society today?

How does 2Corinthians 11:13-14 describe his tactics?

What do we learn about his character?

a. John 8:44

b. John 10:10a

c. 1John 3:8a

4. This man of the tombs met Jesus as soon as He stepped foot out of the boat. His life was destroyed body soul, and spirit; and yet Jesus, knowing his need, made the journey across the sea for one purpose, and one purpose only – to deliver this demon-possessed man. As believers in Jesus Christ, we have no need to fear the enemy. He has no power to possess or control. We have the Holy Spirit dwelling in our lives and have been given everything we need to have victory against his attacks on our life. How do the following Scriptures remind you of your responsibility and ability to walk in victory?

a. Ephesians 6:11-18

b. 1John 4:4

c. James 4:7

What three "R's" are we given that we must always remember and practice when we approach anything that has to do with Jesus?

1.

2.

3.

What does Luke 8:28-29 teach us about the power and authority of Jesus, and how will it affect your walk today?

What did it take for this man to be set free from the legion of enemies?

They knew their dismiss was certain. What was the request of the enemy? What happened?

According to Luke 8:34, what was the response of those who were feeding the swine?

5. Seeing what happened, the herdsmen were certainly frightened, and they ran to gather witnesses. What amazing sight did they behold when they returned?

What does Luke 8:35-36 tell us about the state of the "former" man of the tombs?

How did the citizens of the region of the Gadarenes respond to this miracle?

Why would someone who had witnessed such an amazing miracle be "seized with great fear?"

Instead of fearing the Lord in the sense of wanting to believe and follow Him, they wanted to get rid of Him because His power and authority were a tremendous threat to their way of life. Jesus showed them a mighty miracle. He knocked on the door of their hearts, but they refused to open. Instead they sent Him away. How does Jesus extend His grace and mercy yet again in His response to the request of the man who had been made whole?

What mission and commission did He give to His newest follower? What report are we given about his progress?

How does it compare to your calling according to 2Corinthians 5:18-21?

Chapter 45
The Desperate Find Jesus – Luke 8:40-56
(Matthew 9:18-26; Mark 5:21-43)

Always begin every Bible Study with prayer. It is the Holy Spirit Who is your Teacher.

1. Read Luke 8:40-56.

2. Read The Jesus Chronicles Chapter 45 (Pages 235-240).

3. After healing the man from Gadera, Jesus returned to Capernaum. What was His reception like, and who was desperately seeking His help?

What was the dire circumstance in the life of Jairus, a ruler of the synagogue, and what would it have cost Him to openly seek Jesus' assistance?

How do the following Scriptures add detail to what this decision meant in Jairus' life?

a. John 9:18-22

b. John 12:42-43

c. John 19:38

How do the following exhortations encourage you in your walk with Jesus as you in the face major trials of life?

a. Psalm 27:1

b. Proverbs 29:25

c. Isaiah 51:7-8

4. God paints a picture of very desperate lives in Luke 8:41-44. What do Matthew 9 and Mark 5 include that tell us how critical the situation was?

As the crowds crushed Jesus and Jairus, what do we learn about the woman who believed she just needed to touch Jesus?

Like Jairus, this woman had also run out of options. What did she do that was very different from Jairus' public display of faith?

What happened that she certainly did not expect?

According to Luke 8:48, what was it that brought healing in this woman's life?

What does Matthew 10:32-33 tells us about why it was absolutely necessary that this woman not be able to slip away in the crowd?

How can you apply this truth to a specific area of your life where you ought to more boldly declare your faith in Jesus?

5. As Jesus stood and spoke with the woman, the most horrible news arrived from Jairus' home. What happened, and what was Jesus' immediate response directly to Jairus?

How often we need to hear these words whispered to our heart. "Do not be afraid, only believe." Literally, "Keep trusting Jesus." How hard is this act of faith in the face of tragedy! What do we learn about the importance of keeping our faith firmly fixed on Jesus?

a. Psalm 37:3-5

b. Proverbs 3:5-8

c. Lamentations 3:25, 26

What amazing miracle took place when Jesus arrived at Jairus' home? How does Jesus describe this little girl upon His arrival?

What does He mean by the word sleeping?

Why do you think Jesus told them not to tell anyone? Do you think they could keep this a secret?

If you are a believer in Jesus Christ, you also have to be raised from the dead and given new life. Whom do you need to tell? Will you? There are lots of desperate folks out there!

Chapter 46
Another Opportunity Lost – Mark 6:1-6
(Matthew 13:54-58; Luke 4:16-24)

Always begin every Bible Study with prayer. It is the Holy Spirit Who is your Teacher.

1. Read Mark 6:1-6.

2. Read The Jesus Chronicles Chapter 46 (Pages 241-244).

3. What two lessons do we learn from Jesus' return to His hometown of Nazareth?

How does it encourage you in your walk today knowing that the Lord will not give up on you?

When did Jesus go to teach?

What was the response of those who heard Him speak?

What about Him astonished those who heard Him in the synagogue?

Read Luke 4:16-24. What details does Luke add about this Sabbath Day message in Nazareth?

4. There was certainly something different about the teaching of this man, Jesus. His insights and interpretation of the Scriptures, and the ideas He expounded, stopped people in their tracks. He spoke exactly to their needs. Yet, they had a problem. According to Mark 6:3, what was it?

What was their response?

What is the Greek word for the word that is translated "offended" in verse 3? What is the definition?

When it comes to human relationships, the saying that "familiarity breeds contempt" is absolutely correct. Why did the people think Jesus could not be the Messiah He claimed to be?

What was Jesus' response to their unbelief?

As believers, what is the danger of familiarity?

We need to guard against taking our walk with the Lord for granted. We cannot allow our joy to wane in the familiarity of the habit. We cannot continue in the motions while allowing the emotion to die off. In Revelation 3:14-17, what stern warning did Jesus give to a church who had forgotten to keep their priorities in check?

According to Revelation 3:18-19, what was His counsel to this lukewarm church?

5. What do we learn about Jesus' ministry among the people in Nazareth?

What was the reason for His lack of miracles?

Jesus marveled at the people's unbelief. What in your life causes God to marvel?

The people's unbelief hindered the work Jesus wanted to accomplish. Did their unbelief make Him unable?

Or did their lack of faith make Him unwilling?

Jesus marveled at the unbelief of the people of Nazareth because He gave them God's Word, yet they didn't hear it. He wanted to do so much more. He came to bring life, but few would listen. He is the same yesterday, today, and forever. He wants to bring life to you through His Word. Will you believe?

How does the prayer of a desperate father from Mark 9:23, 24 resonate to those seemingly impossible circumstances in your life?

Will you choose to trust Him today? When you do, He will be free to work great miracles in your life!

Chapter 47
Learning to Serve By His Power – Mark 6:7-13
(Matthew 10:1-42; Luke 9:1-6)

Always begin every Bible Study with prayer. It is the Holy Spirit Who is your Teacher.

1. Read Mark 6:7-13.

2. Read The Jesus Chronicles Chapter 47 (Pages 245 - 248).

3. In Mark 6, we are coming to the end of Jesus' one-and-a half-year ministry in Galilee. His last year would be spent heading south into Jerusalem and the surrounding areas. Jesus was taking His disciples from learning to doing. What was their mission according to Mark 6: 7?

Why did He send them out two-by-two?

Where did the power come from that allowed them to succeed in the ministry?

Was Jesus more concerned about the results of their work or their willingness to go and serve?

How does the commissioning of Moses in Exodus 4:10-12 address our excuses about not being able to be an effective witness?

What does John 14:26-27 add that encourages you to surrender your will to Jesus' direction each day?

4. Notice that the Lord equipped and empowered the disciples. What is the definition of the word translated power in Mark 6:7?

How do the following Scriptures speak of the same power? How is it absolutely essential in your walk today?

a. Acts 1:8

b. Romans 15:18-19

c. 1 Corinthians 2:4

d. 1 Thessalonians 1:5

It is the Holy Spirit's work not only to save us, but also to prepare us to serve God. Christianity differs from all other religions in that the Lord calls us and equips us. What important truth do we learn from the following verses?

a. John 15:5

b. Philippians 4:13

5. As Jesus sent out these twelve, He gave them a very specific task. What were their instructions?

What was the reason for the very limited resources the disciples were to take on their journey?

What promise do we have of His abundant provision in our lives?

a. 2Corinthians 9:8-11

b. Philippians 4:19

What lesson can we learn about how we are to deal with the rejection of those who refuse to hear the truth of the Gospel?

How is John 15:18-20 an encouragement to you in your walk today?

Jesus sent out His disciples with some parting words. Where were they to stay, and when were they to go?

Verses 12-13 give us a summary of the ministry of the disciples as they went out in faith to share the Good News. What were the results?

Chapter 48
Death of a Conscience – Mark 6:14-29
(Matthew 14:1-14; Luke 9:7-9)

Always begin every Bible Study with prayer. It is the Holy Spirit Who is your Teacher.

1. Read Mark 6:14-29.

2. Read The Jesus Chronicles Chapter 48 (Pages 249-254).

3. We are coming closer to the final year of Jesus' public ministry. Soon He would head south to Jerusalem and the cross. Our attention is turned from the disciples' commission to the man, King Herod. Who was he, and what had he done that made him concerned about Jesus' presence in the Galilee?

   Who did King Herod believe Jesus was?

   The disciples had been sent out in pairs so there were six cities at any given time in the Galilee area that had someone preaching Jesus. His name had become well known, and most had an opinion about who He was.
   What were the popular opinions?

   Who is Jesus, and why did He come?

   a. John 3:16, 17

   b. John 10:27, 28

c. John 11:25, 26

d. John 14:6

4. Herod's sin was uncovered by the ministry of John the Baptist, and he was still imprisoned by guilt, which was exposed when he heard of the miracle claim about Jesus. When confronted with our sinfulness, we really have only two options. What are they?

According to Psalm 32:3-4, what was David's life like when he was hiding his sin?

Record David's confession from Psalm 51:3-12.

What amazing promise does 1 John 1:9 give that will encourage you today?

The conscious awareness of sin is certainly a gift of God. Why, and what will it do in your heart?

According to 1 Timothy 4:1-3, what extreme danger is there to the one who constantly rejects the conviction of the conscience?

5. It was a year and a half earlier, when John declared Herod's marriage to Herodias sinful. Herodias was furious. What does Mark 6:20 say about Herod's opinion of John the Baptist?

God's Word, delivered by John, had two completely different effects on Herodias and Herod. Herod's conscience was stirred, he listened and "heard him gladly." But, what did he fail to do over the course of time?

What warning is given in Hebrews 3:12-15 about the importance of making a decision about the Lord?

As Herod delayed to make a commitment, Herodias continued to plot against John the Baptist. Herod found himself in a horrible dilemma that produced great distress. There is a decision point in every person's life. If we delay to choose, our heart will become hardened. At some point the Lord will no longer strive with man. What exhortation did Joshua give to the children of Israel in Joshua 24:15-16?

John the Baptist was a very simple, faithful, courageous, righteous man who ministered to a very flamboyant, foul man who had no spine. John lost his head but kept his life. Herod lost everything! In Mark 6:14, how did Herod compare the works of Jesus with what he remembered about John?

He still had a chance to repent. Did he?

What are the details of the last meeting between Herod and Jesus according to Luke 23:7-9?

Maybe the most telltale sign of Herod's dead conscience was that Jesus had nothing more to say to him. It was too late for Herod. Today is the day of salvation. If you are His child, you should be telling everyone you meet. According to 2Corinthians 5:20-21, what is your mission, and what is your message?

Chapter 49
I'm Your Sufficiency – Mark 6:30-44
(Matthew 14:13-21; Luke 9:10-17; John 6:5-13)

Always begin every Bible Study with prayer. It is the Holy Spirit Who is your Teacher.

1. Read Mark 6:30-44.

2. Read The Jesus Chronicles Chapter 49 (Pages 255-260).

3. What was the circumstance of this day on the hills of Galilee that gave great opportunity for the disciples to learn an important lesson?

What is the lesson?

How can you apply this lesson to a seemingly impossible circumstance in your life?

Throughout this account of Jesus amongst the people, what do we learn about His heart for this huge crowd of followers?

According to Mark 6:31, what was Jesus' suggestion to the disciples who had recently returned from a ministry trip?

What occurred instead?

According to verse 34, what is Jesus' heart toward the lost and needy?

What is the definition of the word compassion in verse 34?

4. How does the disciples' attitude toward the hopeless and needy compare to their Lord's? What was their solution to the problem of the hungry crowd?

Jesus had immediately set about caring for the sheep by teaching them about salvation and life. What does Luke add in Luke 9:11?

So the disciples watched Jesus minister to the people with great joy while they steamed at how they were losing precious personal time. What was Jesus' response in Mark 6:37 to the disciples plan to "send them away?

According to John 6:6, why did the Lord give the disciples this seemingly impossible command?

What do we learn about the "impossible" from Matthew 19:26?

Record Jeremiah 32:27. Do you believe it?

5. We should learn from this text that when God puts us in a place where our faith is tried or where our knowledge of God is put to the test, it is never for His benefit, but always for ours. What is the purpose of the trials in our lives?

    a. Romans 5:3, 4

    b. 2Corinthians 4:16-18

    c. James 1:2-4

Phillip and Andrew (and all the other disciples for that matter) failed to remember that standing before them was Jesus, who is the Bread of Life. They sought to solve the matter, finding their resources far too small and the problem far too huge. They had no answer. Who had the most faith amongst the characters in this account?

What did he do and why?

Notice that the insufficient from the hands of the insignificant becomes both sufficient and significant the moment it passes through Jesus' hands. What was the outcome of this miracle that is recorded in every one of the Gospel records?

How does it keep you from excusing yourself because you don't think you have enough to offer?

Think about it. Nothing is too hard for your Heavenly Father. Will you trust Him today with the "impossible" in your life?

Chapter 50
Storm Sense – Mark 6:45-56
(Matthew 14:22-36; John 6:15-21)

Always begin every Bible Study with prayer. It is the Holy Spirit Who is your Teacher.

1. Read Mark 6:45-56.

2. Read The Jesus Chronicles Chapter 50 (Pages 261-266).

3. Jesus had just fed thousands. What was left over after this miracle?

What lesson was learned from these abundant leftovers?

Why did Jesus quickly send the disciples away? What was the plan of the crowd and why?

What did He do when He departed from the crowd?

How does Jesus' example in the following Scriptures encourage you to spend the needed time in prayer?

a. Mark 1:35

b. Luke 6:12

What do the following references teach us about how we must incorporate prayer in our lives?

a. Matthew 6:6

b. Romans 8:26

c. James 5:13-16

4. The crowds were pressing in and demanding to see Jesus. They were not seeking Him for spiritual reasons but for what they could get from Him. He departed to the mountains to pray. What did Jesus observe as He watched His disciples attempting to obey His command?

How far had the disciples rowed the boat?

What does the word "straining" in Mark 6:48 tell us about the effort they were exerting?

What was on the boat the entire time they were rowing that stood as a reminder of what they (and we) ought to do first when we are in the midst of a storm?

The disciples were determined to obey, but they were trying to do it in their own strength. What should they have done?

What does John 15:5 tell us about the only way we are able to walk in victory?

5. What is the purpose of the storms that Jesus allows in our lives?

It takes time to learn to trust God in the storm. Read Matthew 14:28-29. What faithful request did Peter make when He saw Jesus walking on the water?

When His eyes were on Jesus, Peter walked. What was the immediate result when he turned his focus from Jesus to the storm?

Is there a circumstance or a person in your life that has distracted you and caused you to take your eyes off of Jesus?

What was the immediate result when Jesus entered the boat?

According to Mark 6:52, why had the disciples missed the lesson?

Immediately upon His arrival at the seashore, the crowds began gathering to Jesus. How did Jesus respond to those who came to seek Him?

How does Psalm 37:5 summarize the lesson of our text today?

Chapter 51
Jesus: The Bread of Life – John 6:22-71
(Matthew 8:19-22; 10:36; 16:13-20;
Mark 8:27-30; Luke 9:18-21)

Always begin every Bible Study with prayer. It is the Holy Spirit Who is your Teacher.

1. Read John 6:22-71.

2. Read The Jesus Chronicles Chapter 51 (Pages 267-276).

3. The crowd that wanted to make Jesus king had traversed around the lake or sailed across to seek Jesus. What was it that the majority of them were looking for?

The crowd found Jesus and asked Him how He had gotten there. Jesus immediately turned the crowds' attention back to their need by asking them a key question, "Why are you here?" It is a question that each of us needs to answer for ourselves, "Why are we doing what we are doing?"

What important lesson do we learn from John 6:26 regarding our motives for seeking and serving?

What peace and comfort do you find in John 6:27? Is there some change that needs to be made in your attitude or priorities in order to be more obedient to Jesus' command?

What encouragement and instruction is given to us in the following Scriptures?

a. Deuteronomy 6:5

b. Matthew 6:31-33

c. Luke 10:40-42

4. What is wrong with the question the crowd asked Jesus in John 6:28?

Why do you think we are so inclined to want to do something, or work our way to Jesus?

Instead, what is required to obtain eternal life (John 6:29)?

Cite a specific Scripture that you could share with someone to support your answer.

This hard-hearted crowd was seeking a sign to prove that Jesus was Who He claimed to be. What definitive statement did He make in John 6:35?

How would you explain what He meant to someone who asked you about this first declaration of I AM in the Gospel of John?

5. Reading John 6:37-40, what two points does Jesus make very clear, and how will trusting in these truths make a difference in your faith today?

When John uses the term "the Jews " what does he mean by it?

Who takes the first step in our salvation? How do you know this?

What is our responsibility when we are called?

Record the promise of John 6:47-48. When the enemy whispers in your ear with doubts about your salvation, how will you combat his lies?

How does 1John 5:12-13 support this truth?

The crowd started out talking about manna. Jesus said the manna gives temporary relief. He had come to give much more. He had come to offer us eternal life. What analogy did Jesus make that caused a great clamor in the crowd? What did He mean by "eat My flesh and drink My blood?

How does Jesus explain His meaning in John 6:63?

Even the disciples were confused at this hard saying, and many walked with Him no more. What was Peter's response to Jesus when asked if he would continue to follow?

Is this the conviction of your heart today?

Chapter 52
Truly Clean! – Mark 7:1-23
(Matthew 15:1-20)

Always begin every Bible Study with prayer. It is the Holy Spirit Who is your Teacher.

1. Read Mark 7:1-23.

2. Read The Jesus Chronicles Chapter 52 (Pages 277-282).

3. The ongoing confrontations between Jesus and the religious leaders of His day point out the difference between what man decides the way to God should be versus God's declared way as found in faith in His Son. Can you imagine the hatred that drove these Pharisees and scribes to pursue Jesus? How far had they travelled?

What means of transportation might they have taken?

What was the first complaint against Jesus that they could raise?

What was their motive in challenging Jesus?

Because Mark's Gospel was written primarily to Gentile believers, what explanation does he give about the question at hand?

According to Mark 7:3b, what was the origin of this practice?

4. In Mark 7:6, 7, what was Jesus' reaction to these man-made traditions that hid the grace and mercy of God under the labors of man?

What does the Word teach us about the righteousness of man?

a. Isaiah 64:6

b. Jeremiah 17:9

c. Jeremiah 2:22

d. Psalm 51:5

In what ways were these religious leaders' exalting man-made laws and rejecting God's commandments?

How does the account of Cain and Abel in Genesis 4:3-7 illustrate the necessity of worshipping the Lord in the manner that He has commanded rather than making our own way?

In what ways are these rules of the Pharisees sometimes wrongly practiced in the church today? How about in your life?

5. Religious people are often religiously zealous about religious practices—but there is no conviction of sin, no desire to be saved, and no need for a Savior. Everything is performance driven. What closing argument did Jesus make to the crowd in Mark 7:14-16?

Where does spiritual defilement come from?

How did Peter learn this lesson in Acts 10:9-17?

Between verses 16-17, Jesus and the disciples entered a house and got away from the crowd. What was the disciples' first question?

What list of actions and attitudes are we given in Mark 7:21-22 that proceed from the defiled heart?

The lesson to the Pharisees, the scribes, the crowd, and us is that the problem of sin is in the heart. What is the solution?

a. Ezekiel 36:26

b. John 3:3; 14-17

c. Romans 8:14-16

Final question: Have you been born-again?

Chapter 53
Jesus and Two Gentiles – Mark 7:24-37
(Matthew 15:21-31)

Always begin every Bible Study with prayer. It is the Holy Spirit Who is your Teacher.

1. Read Mark 7:24-37.

2. Read The Jesus Chronicles Chapter 53 (Pages 283-287).

3. After sparring with the scribes and Pharisees, Jesus went northwest to a predominantly Gentile area known as the Decapolis—a place where these religious men from Jerusalem would not follow Him. The crowds were pressing in – they needed a touch from Jesus. Where did Jesus and His disciples go? What were they seeking? What did they find?

What did you learn about the woman who came insistently to get help from Jesus?

How would this woman have been perceived and judged by the religious leaders of Jesus' day?

Religious intolerance isn't new, but it did, and will, occur in all times and nations. What was the request of this persistent Greek, Canaanite woman?

Nothing could deter this woman from coming to Jesus, or keep her away from Him. Why was she seeking Jesus?

How does her persistence encourage you in your seeking of Jesus today?

4. Record Matthew 15:22.

What do we learn about the faith of this woman based on her request to Jesus?

Why did He challenge her in such a strong manner?

If you ever wanted to find someone with a humble heart coming to the Lord, this is certainly one. This Gentile woman came to Jesus solely on the basis of mercy. What was the outcome of this woman's encounter with Jesus?

According to Matthew 15:23, what was the disciples reaction to this persistent woman?

How does their reaction challenge you in how you deal with the hurting and needy that the Lord brings into your life?

How do the following Scriptures encourage you today in how you deal with weak and struggling brethren?

a. Isaiah 35:3, 4

b. 1 Thessalonians 5:14, 15

c. Galatians 6:1, 2

d. Ephesians 4:32

5. Departing from the region of Tyre and Sidon, He came through the midst of the region of the Decapolis to the Sea of Galilee. Amongst this mixture of Jew and Gentiles, Jesus again made Himself known. Who did He meet, and what were the circumstances in this man's life?

Read Isaiah 35. What does it tell you about God's plans for your life?

Why do you think Jesus went into such detail in the healing of the deaf and mute man?

In order to be useful servants for Jesus, we must have hearts that break for the lost. We must be moved by their pain and be fearful for their future. What breaks your heart?

Read Nehemiah 1. What did Nehemiah's broken heart lead him to do?

When Jesus healed the deaf / mute man in Mark 7, what instruction did He give him? Did He obey?

Has Jesus healed your broken life and set you free for eternity? Who will you tell today?

Chapter 54
Nurturing Spiritual Understanding
Mark 8:1-26
(Matthew 15:32-39; 16:1-12)

Always begin every Bible Study with prayer. It is the Holy Spirit Who is your Teacher.

1. Read Mark 8:1-26.

2. Read The Jesus Chronicles Chapter 54 (Pages 288-292).

3. We have come to a series of lessons where the Lord will tell us that although He is very patient with nurturing our spiritual understanding, at some point, we must respond with what we have learned. We need to make progress, grow up, and practice living what we have learned. What took place in Mark 8:1-9 that sounds very familiar to another miraculous event?

What was the crucial lesson that the disciples were so slow to learn?

Have you needed to learn and re-learn the lesson of trusting the Lord to provide what you need?

How would believing and obeying the following Scriptures give you victory?

a. Psalm 37:3-6

b. Proverbs 3:5, 6

c. Isaiah 26:3, 4

d. Jeremiah 17:7, 8

e. Philippians 4:6, 7

4. With this crucial lesson again illustrated, along came the Pharisees and the Sadducees. These two groups had only one thing in common – their hatred for Jesus. Their reason for coming was to chide and discredit. They asked for a sign, as if they had not seen enough miracles. What was Jesus' response to their question in Mark 8:12?

Did they get a sign?

What was Jesus' response to these men who opposed the truth of His Words?

What was the topic of conversation in the boat as Jesus and the disciples crossed the sea?

What did the disciples think Jesus meant by this warning? Could He have multiplied that one loaf of bread if need be?

What does leaven represent in the Bible?

Did they not care, or were they not listening?

What have you permanently learned this year that has affected your life so you'll never be the same? Have you established a "Gilgal" to remind you of God's faithfulness?

5. Finally, they came to Bethsaida. What happened immediately?

How did this healing take place? Why?

Sometimes we need to grow in faith slowly. Our Lord is very patient with the willing weak. Read the story of Gideon in Judges 6-7. What was his sign?

After Jesus healed the blind man, He told him not to go into the town of Bethsaida. Why?

For those around you, there is still time. What are we told about our calling and commission to those who don't yet know Jesus?

a. Mark 16:15, 16

b. 2Corinthians 5:18-21

Selah (think about it)...as though God were pleading through you...who do you need to tell about His love?

Chapter 55
Who Do You Say That I Am? – Luke 9:18-26
(Matthew 16:13-27; Mark 8:27-38)

Always begin every Bible Study with prayer. It is the Holy Spirit Who is your Teacher.

1. Read Luke 9:18-26.

2. Read The Jesus Chronicles Chapter 55 (Pages 293-298).

3. As Jesus neared the end of two and a half years of public ministry spent primarily in the area of the Galilee, how did His message and His behavior change?

What question did Jesus ask His disciples?

What was their answer?

Where did this conversation take place?

What had these folks in the crowd missed when it came to their conclusion about who Jesus was?

Who were they expecting and what did they want to see Jesus do?

According to the Bible, Who takes the first step in the salvation process?

4. One thing is obvious from the disciples' report of what the crowds thought. What is it?

It is clear that the world is not able to label Jesus as a "good man" or "a prophet". Based on His statements about Himself, what are the three conclusions that you can draw about Who He is?

What do the following Scriptures teach us about Who Jesus is?

a. John 6:51

b. John 10:9,10

c. John 10:27, 28

d. John 11:25, 26

e. John 14:6

f. John 17:1-3

5. In Luke 9:20, what was Peter's answer to Jesus' question?

What does Matthew 16:16-17 add to the details of the spiritual revelation that came to Peter?

Peter received spiritual revelation regarding Jesus' identity. What were the means and circumstances by which he understood that Jesus was the Messiah?

In Matthew 16:18, what was Jesus' conclusion about Peter's revelation?

What did He mean by this statement?

In Matthew 16:19 Jesus made a statement that has been misused and misinterpreted. What are the keys of the kingdom of heaven, and what does it mean that the disciples could bind or loosen?

Jesus warned the disciples to keep silent for His time had not yet come. What clear declaration did Jesus make about what His near future healed? (Luke 9:22)

In Luke 9:23-26, what exhortation is given and what challenge is extended regarding the full commitment required in the life of the follower of Jesus Christ?

What is the highest priority in your life? Are you willing to take up the cross and follow Jesus at all costs?

Chapter 56
The Transfiguration – Luke 9:27-36
(Matthew 17:1-8; Mark 9:2-8)

Always begin every Bible Study with prayer. It is the Holy Spirit Who is your Teacher.

1. Read Luke 9:27-36.

2. Read The Jesus Chronicles Chapter 56 (Pages 299-303).

3. Eight days after Peter's declaration at Caesarea Philippi, an event took place that was previously unique to the Old Testament. What happened?

Who went up the mountain with Jesus?

What did they see?

What was different about the appearance of Jesus?

Who else appeared with Him?

What were these three talking about?

4. It is clear from the whole of the Bible that God desires intimate fellowship with His kids. How did He reveal Himself in the following circumstances?

    a. The Exodus from Egypt

    b. With Moses on Mt. Sinai

    c. When Moses asked God to show him His glory

    d. In the building and dedication of the Tabernacle

    e. During the time of Solomon's Temple

    The New Testament opens with the exciting news that God wanted to show the people His glory after 400 years of silence from heaven. Read John 1:1-14. What does this text reveal to you about Who Jesus is?

5. Eight days after Peter's great confession, Jesus took three of His disciples on a hike up a high mountain apart by themselves. As the disciples slept, Jesus prayed! As He prayed, He was transfigured. Standing between Moses the Lawgiver and Elijah the prophet was Jesus Christ – the fulfillment of both. According to Luke 9:32, what did the disciples see when they awoke?

What plan did Peter immediately come up with?

How does Mark 9:6 help explain Peter's plan?

According to Luke 9:34-35, what amazing event occurred as Peter was still speaking?

What declaration did the Father make?

The cloud that had passed by Moses in the cleft, that occupied the tent of meeting, that filled the temple on dedication day, and that slowly moved away from the place of worship was none other than the Son of God Who had now come to give people light. How does Peter describe this event in 2Peter 1:16-18?

Then the voice ceased, the cloud disappeared, and the disciples remained alone with Jesus. Now they knew Him much better. They had seen His glory! What instruction are we given at the end of Luke 9:35?

How can you apply it in your life today?

What instruction is given us in the following Scriptures about the necessity of listening and obeying?

a. John 13:15-17

b. John 15:10

c. James 1:23-25

God does not forsake His people. He is available. If you want to know Him, look to Jesus. If you want life, follow Him. How bright is the light that is shining in your life?

Chapter 57
True Greatness – Luke 9:37-50
(Matthew 17:14-23, 18:1-6; Mark 9:14-40)

Always begin every Bible Study with prayer. It is the Holy Spirit Who is your Teacher.

1. Read Luke 9:37-50.

2. Read The Jesus Chronicles Chapter 57 (Pages 304-308).

3. As the time drew closer for Jesus to turn south and head directly for Jerusalem and the cross, He continued to prepare His disciples to be those through whom He would do His work in years to come. What is God's purpose for us as He leaves us in this world?

What happened as Jesus and the disciples came down from the mountaintop experience?

What do we learn about the advantages and challenges of the mountaintop experience? Why?

What is our purpose in this world as Christians?

a. Matthew 5:14-16

b. Philippians 2:14-16

c. 1 Peter 2:9

4. Who came seeking Jesus when He came down from the mountain?

What was his request?

What had this father tried that had failed?

Why had the disciples failed to cast out the demon?

What did Jesus do when He encountered the possessed child?

How does Luke 9:43 describe the crowd's reaction when Jesus healed the child?

"The majesty of God" is the same phrase Peter used later to describe the Transfiguration. As Jesus healed the demon-possessed boy, the crowds witnessed the glory that Peter, James, and John had seen on the mountain. What did Jesus reveal in Luke 9:43-45 about His future? How did the disciples respond?

5. Even after being eyewitnesses to miracle after miracle, the disciples argued. What was their dispute over?

What illustration did Jesus give regarding those who are the greatest and the least among us?

Do you want to be great? What do you need to do?

a. Isaiah 57:15

b. Matthew 23:11, 12

c. Philippians 2:3-6

d. 1 Peter 5:5, 6

The disciples' dispute about who was the greatest led to another issue we need to beware of allowing in our lives. What is it?

God will use those who depend on Him and will bless those who are in fellowship with Him regardless of their denominational label. How did Moses address this same issue in Numbers?

What did Paul have to say about this ministry rivalry in Philippians 1:15-18?

How can you specifically guard against it in your walk with Jesus?

Chapter 58
The Stage Is Set – Matthew 18:1-14
(Mark 9:33-50; Luke 9:46-50, 15:3-7)

Always begin every Bible Study with prayer. It is the Holy Spirit Who is your Teacher.

1. Read Matthew 18:1-14.

2. Read The Jesus Chronicles Chapter 58 (Pages 309-311).

3. We have come to the end of Jesus' first two and a half years of public ministry. What are the remaining Gospel records devoted to?

What was the lengthy conversation that caused the disciples to ask the question, "Who then is the greatest in the kingdom of heaven?"

The discussion in this chapter is stern in many ways, but it also reveals to us God's heart for the church and how we are to relate to one another. According to Jesus' teaching, who then is the greatest in the kingdom of heaven?

What does Jesus mean by, "unless you are converted and you become as little children?"

What do the following Scriptures add?

a. 1 Corinthians 14:20

b. 1 Peter 2:1, 2

4. The instruction is that we are to "humble ourselves" as little children. What does the Word teach us about humility?

a. Isaiah 57:15

b. Luke 18:13, 14

c. 1 Peter 5:5-7

d. James 4:8-10

Jesus tells us that we can be certain that offenses will come. In Matthew 18:6, 7, what strong warning is given to anyone who would cause the child of God to stumble and sin?

Do a word search in your Bible, and find another place where the exclamation "woe" is used?

5. Jesus says, "Woe to that man by whom the offenses come." What severe instruction did Jesus give in Matthew 18:8-9? What does it mean?

It is important to notice that, in context, the instruction to "cast off the member that sins" is related to the sin of causing others to stumble. Obviously Jesus' instruction is not to be taken literally. The issue is the length to which you should go to be sure you are not causing others to veer off course in their walk with the Lord. What do we learn from the following Scriptures that will protect us from harming God's kids?

a. Zechariah 2:8

b. Romans 14:13-15

c. 1 Corinthians 8:9-13

d. 1 John 2:10

According to Matthew 18:10, what added protection do we have as God's children?

Jesus closes our text with an illustration of the shepherd and his flock. What is the lesson?

How does this truth cause you to rejoice to the Great Shepherd's care in your life?

So rather than fault finding with our brethren, what are we to do that pleases the heart of our Father?

Chapter 59
Church Discipline
Matthew 18:15-22

Always begin every Bible Study with prayer. It is the Holy Spirit Who is your Teacher.

1. Read Matthew 18:15-22.

2. Read The Jesus Chronicles Chapter 59 (Pages 312-317).

3. After establishing the truths that causing God's children to stumble is a bad idea and that the heart of the Father is to restore those who are straying, Jesus went on to give us the most definitive verses in the Bible on church discipline and church relationships. Describe the first step in the reconciliation process.

   Who should be involved?

   What is the goal?

   How often should we seek to make contact?

   If you have become involved in restoration only to be shunned, refused, and maligned, what do you do next?

   Who do you take with you?

If repeated efforts fail, it becomes necessary to involve the church leadership. The church cannot be a safe harbor for sin. These are the hardest steps, and it presumes that lots of work has been done beforehand. What is still the purpose in this process?

4. How does Matthew 18:18-20 apply to this process of restoration?

How would it be an encouragement to church leaders who have to make hard decisions in obedience to the Lord and protection of the flock of God?

Jesus promises to support and stand by the difficult decisions that sometimes need to be made regarding those who call themselves saints but are living sinful lives. What do the terms bind and loose mean in Matthew 18:18?

How is this same concept used in the following Scriptures?

a. Luke 24:46-48

b. John 20:22, 23

Just for the record, does Matthew 18:20 have anything to do with prayer or your prayer life?

5. What question did Peter ask the Lord about the subject of forgiveness?

Peter probably thought he was willing to forgive far above the expected demands. What was Jesus' response?

Have you been practicing seventy times seven in your walk with the Lord?

One of the interesting things about forgiveness from God's point of view is that He never asks of us any more than He's given us. What do we learn from the following Scriptures about the command of our Lord to walk in forgiveness?

a. Ephesians 4:32

b. Colossians 3:12, 13

c. Mark 11:25, 26

d. 1 Peter 3:8, 9

When we think it is too much to ask that we be willing to forgive those who offend us, we must consider our example and think about Jesus at Calvary. Read Luke 23:33, 34.

Every step of discipline has to be taken in light of support and restoration. That's God's desire. Are you willing to be a part of that restorative process?

Chapter 60
The Parable of the Unforgiving Servant
Matthew 18:23-35

Always begin every Bible Study with prayer. It is the Holy Spirit Who is your Teacher.

1. Read Matthew 18:23-35.

2. Read The Jesus Chronicles Chapter 60 (Pages 318-321).

3. In the last portion of this chapter that deals with the way the church is to interact, Jesus tells a parable. What is the subject?

What is the eternal lesson?

Read Matthew 18:26 & 29. What was the cry for mercy in the heart of both these men?

What does the phrase "kingdom of heaven" most often speak of?

The first servant begged for mercy. What was the Master's response?

How have you seen this forgiveness at work in your life? Be specific?

4. What do the following Scriptures command us to do as followers of Jesus?

a. Matthew 6:14, 15

b. Luke 6:37

c. 1 Peter 2:20-25

d. 1 Peter 3:8-11

Facing the imminent loss of everything he counted valuable, this first servant in Matthew 18 didn't ask for justice. What did he ask for? What was it he truly needed?

The fortunate thing in the whole picture is that this king is a good king, a loving king, a "for you" not an "against you" king – a king who came to save, not destroy. What encouragement do you find in Jeremiah 29:11-13 that will help you when it "seems" there is no way to make it through the trials in your life?

How does Psalm 86:5 show us the character of our Heavenly Father?

When God's love meets the inescapable judgment of sin and produces a new life, it's an awesome picture. This first servant did not need more time; he needed forgiveness of his debt. What promise are we given in 1John 1:7-9 about the extent of forgiveness offered to us through the Lord Jesus Christ?

5. What happens next in our parable seems unthinkable. What amazing choice did the forgiven servant make?

Peter thought seven times was an efficient amount of forgiveness. What was Jesus' answer?

Read Luke 6:27-36. Who is there in your life that might fall into the category of your enemy in some form or another?

What are you called to do to them, and for them? Review Luke 6:37 from question #4. What does it command about forgiveness? Why?

The lesson is obvious. Whatever debt you will ever be required to forgive someone else will pale in comparison to the debt God has forgiven you. What, then, is the basis for restoration among brethren?

Who saw this harsh treatment, and what action did they take?

According to Matthew 18:34, how did the master respond, and what action did he take?

What is the price of unforgiveness in the life of a believer? Will you lose your salvation? What will you lose?

Record Matthew 18:35 and determine before the Lord Jesus Christ to choose forgiveness!